Surprised by Hope

Surprised by Hope

From Circus Girl to Quadriplegic—A Journey through Tragedy to a Promise for Tomorrow

Vickie Baker

HORIZON BOOKS

CAMP HILL, PENNSYLVANIA

HORIZON BOOKS

3825 Hartzdale Drive, Camp Hill, PA 17011
www.cpi-horizon.com
www.christianpublications.com

Surprised by Hope
ISBN: 0-88965-161-2
LOC Catalog Card Number: 99-080159

00   01   02   03   04   5   4   3   2   1

Table of Contents

Part Three: Swing Forward

Part Four: Happy to Be Alive

Part Five: Soaring Again

Acknowledgments

I used to wonder why writers acknowledged so many people in the front of their books. After all, writing is a singular affair, isn't it? Then I became a writer and quickly learned that the never-ending rewrites involve many minds sharper than mine. These sharp minds belong to the people who remind me of important stuff like, "The readers can't read your mind. They only know what you tell them!" Yes, Marlene. . . .

To Gary, my former husband and performing partner who read and re-read chapters, helping me to sort out the tangled emotions of that time.

To my critique group: Janet, Vicki, Darlene, Ruth, Irene, Jean, Laurel, Nancy and Ron, who listened week after week with a critical ear, made hard-hitting suggestions that I did not want to hear and wouldn't let anything slide.

To Marlene Bagnull, a dear friend and writing mentor who exclaimed at my very first writers' conference, "You can really write!" Your suggestions hit even harder! Thanks for believing in me and for corralling my scattered thoughts to shape this book into reality.

To Dr. Lammertse and the staff at Craig Rehabilitation Hospital whose genuine care and concern brought comfort when I first rolled through the doors as a "down in the pits" quadriplegic trapeze artist—and for your encouragement and hands-on help with the writing of this book.

To Mae-Lynne Poland, Pastor Keith, all of my friends behind bars and the countless others who helped introduce me to the one true Ringmaster. Through your actions you have taught me that hope springs eternal, that joy does not depend on circumstances and that the greatest show on earth is yet to come.

And last but not least, to God, who sets my gimpy feet on high places and helps me to stand firm as I hunt and peck for His glory. Without You, there would be no book to write, no point in sticking around, no happy endings. Thank You for not giving up on me when I gave up on myself.

Author's Note: Some of the names in this book have been changed to protect those who really ticked me off.

PART ONE

Rock Bottom

CHAPTER ONE

Stopped Alive in My Tracks

━◆━◆━◆━◆━

At last the torrential downpour subsided, ushering in a cool, overcast night. The stars were somberly shrouded in a grey-white haze. Steamroller clouds played peek-a-boo with the moon until it finally vanished for good. Perfect. No traffic paraded by, no prying lights shone. No neighbors were out for a late night stroll. There was enough of a breeze to boss a nearby screen door back and forth. *Squeak-thump, squeak-thump.* Annoying. *Squeak-thump, squeak-thump.*

The van door slammed shut, blocking out all noise. I embraced the silence. The inviting darkness of the van's interior comforted my jagged nerves. Not a soul stirred. *Good.* Relief cut a narrow channel through my mind. *This time, we'll pull it off.*

My husband dragged his weary frame into the driver's seat. Gary's haggard face, sporting two days' worth of stubble, seemed to have aged ten years these past few months. He looked back at me.

"Ready?"

I nodded. "Let's go."

He turned the key and the van sprang to life, purring quietly.

I lay motionless on a couch behind the driver's seat. A sudden spasm caused my legs to tense up. Bony knees jerked toward me, trembled for a few seconds then became limp. I surveyed my appearance. Ugly fingers: permanently curled inward. Unable to move; unable to function. Toothpick arms: barely enough strength to pick up a piece of popcorn. Puny upper body: couldn't even raise myself into a sitting position or lean forward without toppling over. Scarecrow legs: a joke. Idle feet that no longer held me up. All worthless. Totally worthless.

I remembered the first time I had seen my knees move—ever so slightly—three weeks post-injury. Wide-eyed with excitement, I had immediately buzzed for my nurse. I just knew that I would walk out of that hospital! I'd show those doctors a thing or two. No wheelchair for me, thank you very much. Even after the nurse stated matter-of-factly that muscle spasms, a common occurrence with paralysis, did not signal any return of function, I clung desperately to that tiny ray of hope. I can remember thinking: *Doctors and nurses don't know everything. I will walk again! That young man in Ringling's flying act got better after he broke his neck. He made a complete recovery. He's already flying again! I can do that. It's possible. How can my life go on otherwise?* I constantly forced myself to choke back the chilling "what if's."

As I lay gazing vacantly at the paneled ceiling of the van—three years wiser now, dreams long shattered and a wheelchair a permanent part of my anatomy—I couldn't remember when the "woe is me blues" had boldly marched into the old grey matter to set up permanent residence. My dark, sunken eyes would have given passersby no reason to question my emaciated physical condition. I gazed vacantly at the paneled ceiling, sure we would succeed this time. Third time's the charm, right?

A few months earlier I had learned—firsthand—that a plastic vacuum cleaner hose melts when taped onto an exhaust pipe. With all the stupid TV I'd watched you'd think I would have learned that. This time we had metal tubing. Despite the hasty conception of our present scheme—I couldn't handle my "fast unto death" anymore—I was sure it would work. This time it would work. After a short drive back to Soda Lakes—to that same remote spot where we had failed a couple of months earlier—we would drift into oblivion quietly, painlessly, unnoticed, unmissed.

Suddenly, out of nowhere, the wail of a siren knifed through the silence. Panic numbed my already dull senses. *This can't be happening! Nooo!* Across the street a dog began to howl. Farther away, others joined in mournful protest. A porch light flickered on. A door cautiously opened a crack, and a homeowner curiously gawked.

Gary reluctantly swung the big vehicle over to the curb. I swore under my breath. Angry words followed as uniformed policemen and Gary disagreed. An ambulance roared up, lights flashing, siren blaring. *Wake up, everybody! Come stare at the losers! Free show tonight!*

Officials roughly yanked Gary's hands behind his back and handcuffed him. Their shouting match continued until I heard a car door slam. My turn. Hands picked me up and deposited me on a waiting stretcher, then the ambulance raced away, closely guarding its prey. The patrol car pulled up to the emergency room at the same time as the ambulance.

Flat on my back in the emergency room, helpless as a tiny baby, I stared dully at my new surroundings. Those jerks had just ruined my plan and I couldn't do a thing about it. Why hadn't I held out just a little longer? I'd spent months working out a way that wouldn't involve anyone else—quite a feat for a quadriplegic—and tonight I blew it. Big time.

Is it possible that God has something to do with my still being alive? That maybe there's a reason behind all this?

No way, the voice of evil hissed. *Why would He care about you? It's your own fault you're still alive. But there's time. You'll find a way, Little Circus Girl. You'll find a way.*

What little control I'd had over my life was now completely gone—snatched away by total strangers. I felt like a wounded animal, helpless and afraid. *They shoot horses who break a leg, but they make paralyzed human beings suffer. And what's the point? Life is so meaningless.* The battle in my head raged on.

The noisy, brightly lit room where the ambulance attendants had abandoned me contained two long rows of beds occupied by strangers. Some people had shackles attached to their wrists and ankles. Suicide attempts? Murderers? Victims? I had not seen the inside of an emergency room since my accident three-and-a-half years earlier. The bed straight across from mine held my husband. *Why is he here?* Too much commotion with "white coats" strutting about for us to talk. We exchanged commiserating looks.

The staff must really trust me. They didn't chain me down. They knew full well that a quadriplegic wouldn't get far on foot. The most I could do was fall out of bed and lie motionless on the floor. That wouldn't scare anybody except me. No problem with this one getting away.

Once I noticed the leather restraints on my husband, I felt even worse. Willing to help me end my suffering, he had chosen to die with me rather than face time behind bars. There's no telling what would happen now. I unleashed my fury against a woman who lived 2,000 miles away as I thought about the phone call Gary had made less than an hour earlier to tell his relatives good-bye. His sister-in-law hadn't liked the idea, so—fearing that she would interfere—we had left the house within minutes of Gary's call. *Minutes!* How could we have known she'd call the cops on us?

Just then, a man in a white coat carrying a clipboard strode arrogantly over to my bed and introduced himself. I took an instant dislike to him. His scraggly red beard and condescending tone of voice fit right in with the sour "I'd rather be anywhere else than here talking to a lowlife scum like you" expression on his tired face.

You aren't the only one who doesn't want to be here, pal!

Dr. Gloom, as I referred to him in the endless days ahead, carefully recorded my answers to his stupid questions. Finally, he told me to sign a piece of paper, which I did by holding his pen in my mouth. Sometime later an orderly wheeled me into another room and I learned that I had just voluntarily signed myself into the psychiatric ward of this hospital for the next seventy-two hours.

I guess it's pretty easy to lie to someone who's half delirious, half starved and half dead. How in the world did I wind up here? And what do I do about it?

CHAPTER TWO

Rolling Nowhere

◆━◆━◆━◆━◆

Where am I? Jail? Lying on an uncomfortably hard mattress in a dimly lit room, I tried to piece together the puzzle. A small sliver of light spilled through torn curtains. Lights twinkled in the distance: traffic lights, headlights, street lights. Freedom—so close, yet so far away. The odor of stale sweat filled the air like a thick fog. My blurry eyes refused to focus. My groggy mind drew a blank. Three narrow beds, each topped with a sheet-covered lump, huddled nearby. The lump directly across from me snored, but it was too high-pitched to be a Gary snore.

Fragments from last night swirled through the hazy confusion in my mind. *Sirens and police yelling at Gary; hands—lots of strange hands, taking me where I did not want to go, holding me hostage in a crowded room. Was that nasty man in a white coat a figment of my imagination? Straps—there were brown leather straps. Oh, no—Gary tied down! They got him. They got him.*

Fear left a bitter, metallic taste in my dry mouth. *And now it's all over. I blew it big time. I'm still alive!*

Faint voices murmured outside the door. Suddenly, from out of nowhere, lights blinded me. The intrusion seemed to penetrate my very soul. An enormous man lurking in the shadows leered at me. I gasped and jerked my head up. He smirked. *What . . . a guard?*

Moments later, the stranger, smug grin and all, vanished from sight—only to return again and again. It felt like I was reliving the same bad dream over and over. Each time he startled me, Mr. "Lord It Over the Crazy Folk with His Flashlight" seemed quite proud of himself. I fought back tears.

Exhausted, yet too wired to sleep, I stared at the wall. A bulletin board adorned with five red tacks hung askew. Mindlessly, I traced a lopsided star using the tacks as points.

Disturbing thoughts bombarded my sluggish senses, thoughts that sent me spinning in circles. *Now what? What can I do now? They ruined it. They ruined everything.*

You can't let them do that, the evil voice whispered in my muddled mind.

But what can I do? I whined. *I can't even move.*

Think, idiot, think! You're stuck here for . . . what . . . seventy-two hours? Three days? That's easy. When they let you out, finish the job. Until then, do what they say. Play by the rules—even if it means eating. Remember, freedom is only three days away.

But Gary. . . .

You don't need him. You don't need anyone, the voice of evil reassured. *You can pull it off by yourself, Little Circus Girl.*

But what if I can't? What if there's no way out? My mind went ballistic as the argument continued. At last, exhaustion won out and I dozed fitfully.

Daylight didn't improve the looks of the room, and what I saw scared me. I squeezed my eyes shut and slowly opened them again. *What's wrong with my eyes?* At least six pairs of enormous curtains—"institution" scrawled all over their orange and green flowers—swam in circles before me. When I turned away, half a dozen bulletin boards met my startled gaze. The tacks jiggled whenever I turned my head. Dozens of empty beds filled the rest of the crowded room. *Where is everyone? There were people in here last night, weren't there?*

I looked up and saw IV stands and lines leading into my left wrist. *When did those go in?* Following the lines to the top of the poles, I spied multiple bags of clear fluid. Just then, a bevy of identical nurses bustled into the room carrying identical trays.

"Hi! I'm Toni," they said in unison. "I'll be your nurse today."

"My nurse?" I mumbled to all of them. "Jails have nurses?"

Toni laughed. I couldn't remember the last time I'd heard such a joyous sound. I hadn't found humor in anything for a long time.

"You're not in jail," Toni said. "This is a hospital. You're on the psychiatric floor. We're going to take real good care of you. I brought you some breakfast. . . . Say, is something wrong? You keep tilting your head to one side."

Watch what you say. I held my head still. "Ah, it's nothing. My eyes are a little out of focus, that's all." My halting answer seemed to satisfy all of them.

"I brought you some orange juice, scrambled eggs, bacon and toast," Toni continued. "Tonight you can fill out a menu for tomorrow's breakfast."

You bet.

"I'll raise the head of your bed." Toni disappeared from view and pushed a button.

"Stop—that's too much!" The walls turned grey right before I passed out. Consciousness returned only after Toni had lowered the bed nearly as much as she'd raised it.

"That's better," I croaked.

"What do you need me to do, hon? Can you feed yourself?"

"Um, no. I'm not sitting up high enough and I don't have a cuff here."

Toni gave me a blank look.

"It's something I strap onto my hand to hold a fork or spoon in place. . . ." My voice trailed off as the thought struck me: *She doesn't know the first thing about spinal cord injury! Does anyone?* A chill raced through me.

"I don't have a lot of time," Toni confided, "but we can get started, anyway." She laid a towel over my gown and carefully loaded a plastic fork with scrambled eggs. I dutifully opened my mouth, chewed and swallowed my first bite of real food in nearly nine weeks.

"Oh, man. I must be losing it."

Toni set the fork down. "What's wrong?"

"It—it tastes good," I said. "It tastes good! This is the first time food has tasted good since my accident."

"That's great!" Toni said. "How long ago was your accident?"

"A little over three years."

Toni picked up a piece of bacon. I opened wide. The flavor—indescribable—almost made me think twice about my plans. Then the emptiness I'd tried so hard to escape crept back into my soul and I came to my senses. *Whether breakfast tastes good or not, life is still pointless. I'll never be able to go back on the road. I'll never be happy.* After the next few bites my stomach said, *Stop!*

"I can't eat any more," I said, eyeing the last savory strip of bacon with regret. "I'm full."

"Here, then. Have some more juice," Toni urged. "We need to keep up on your fluid intake."

Play the game, Vickie. Just play the game. I dutifully finished the juice. Toni wiped off my mouth and picked up the tray. "Can you reach your call switch?" she asked.

"My fingers don't work so I won't be able to use a regular—" I stopped mid-sentence and stared at the odd-looking device.

"A light touch should activate it," Toni explained. "Try it."

I tapped the surface with the back of my gimpy right hand. A light flashed on above the door.

"You got it," Toni said. "I'll be back to give you a bed bath after I check on my other patients. Need anything before I go?"

"Yes. Will you tell me why someone kept shining lights in my eyes all night?"

Toni set the tray down. "Your doctor put you on a suicide watch. That means that someone has to check on you every half hour."

"Huh? What does he think I can do? I can't even turn over in bed without help." *I'm totally at their mercy—ridiculous lights and all—and I can't do a thing about it.* I could feel the noose tightening. *Life can't get any worse.*

"You rest now, hon."

I closed my eyes, but a few minutes later a sick feeling in the pit of my stomach gave warning and my bowels let loose—a pattern that would repeat itself many times in the days to come. *I lied. Things can get worse.*

Toni soon returned carrying a basin, some towels and a fresh gown.

"Ah, breakfast didn't agree with me," I said wishing myself invisible. Toni pulled back the covers.

"I'm sorry," I muttered. "What a mess."

"Don't worry about it, hon. I'll get you cleaned up in a flash." When she finished filling the basin with warm water, Toni brought over a stack of clean washcloths and towels. She turned me on my side. I rolled back.

"You need to put a pillow behind my back," I said. "That's the only way I'll stay put. And one between my knees—so I don't get any red marks."

"I'll be right back," Toni said. "Don't go anywhere."

Yeah, right.

Her hasty trip to the supply closet yielded pillows, fresh linens, a new sheepskin to help prevent bed sores and another nurse to help change the sheets. Together, they finished cleaning me up.

"Comfy?" Toni asked.

"Fine." A huge yawn escaped me.

"Why don't you take a nap? I'll check on you later. Oh, before I forget, let's fill out your lunch menu." After she circled my choices, Toni left, making sure to place the call device within reach. No sooner had she disappeared than a man in a white coat trudged through the door. The hair on the back of my neck bristled. Something familiar, yet very disturbing, about his presence spoke fear to my heart.

I know this guy, don't I? But how? My heart raced as he approached and a nameless fear gripped me. Tension charged the air. His eyes remained downcast. His face appeared unshaven, his red hair, uncombed. When he reached the bed, he looked up. I gasped.

So I didn't just imagine you. Last night's "figment of my imagination," Dr. Gloom, towered over me and talked down to me—a true "god-doc." His "holier than thou" expression conveyed superiority and pity. *Welcome to Dirtbag Patient 101, Vickie.* His patronizing voice droned on.

Sometime later, I watched him trudge back out the door. *What on earth did we just talk about? I wish Gary was here. I wish I knew where he was.* Before many tears could squeeze out, I nodded off.

Gary and I gracefully style to the audience, remove our capes and turn toward the rigging. We climb up the ladder while a prop-hand holds tension at the bottom. Our catcher ascends as far as the net and bounces his way across. He raises his body up a thick rope—hand over hand—to the catch trapeze. Amidst circus music and applause, the act progresses smoothly until I perform my two-and-a-half.

My headfirst landing jerked me awake before I could sink down into the net. It always did.

"Hello, honey."

Startled, I looked up. "Oh, hi, Mom. Hi, Dad."

Conversation followed familiar channels—nice, safe, surface talk of some sort until my question rocked the boat.

"Where's Gary? Is he OK? What have they done to him?"

My silent father turned and stared out the window—his typical "ignore the problem and it will go away" response. Just don't cause waves.

My mother's frown spoke volumes. She had reached her verdict about Gary months ago. Now it just remained for her to convince me of how I should feel.

My questions hung suspended in midair like a trapeze artist who's just released the flybar and hasn't yet connected with the catcher. But I didn't see any catchers in sight. Shoot, I didn't even spot a safety net.

Next thing I knew, an empty room swam into focus, silent as a tomb. *When did I fall asleep? Did Mom and Dad go home? And what happened to Gary?* I could no longer hold back the tears.

It's not fair! my mind screamed. *It's just not fair! My body is screwed up for life because of a split-second mistake in timing. My husband is locked up—only God knows where. And I'm stuck here because I can't even kill myself right.*

PART TWO

Swing Back

CHAPTER THREE

Swinging Bars

◆━◆━◆━◆━◆

The following morning began with Dr. Gloom's patronizing voice, tired face and stupid questions. Year? 1987. Date? August 22. President? Reagan. Now count backward from 100 by sevens. . . .

Next, a cold breakfast arrived, served by an equally cold nurse. The meal ended with the same results as yesterday. After the nurse cleaned me up, I stared at the walls. No roommates reappeared after breakfast. No husband popped in. I felt like a prisoner sentenced to solitary confinement. My restless mind wandered.

When the piercing emptiness threatened to close in around me, I escaped to the past—back to when the circus swept me off my feet.

It started nine years ago when a skydiving friend invited me to try trapeze at the YMCA downtown.

I almost chickened out. The thought of traipsing into a room full of strangers practically made me gag. But finally, after promising myself that I would leave if I didn't find Sue, I marched resolutely toward the building. Once inside, my feet transported me to the main desk. After paying a modest fee, I headed for the gymnasium.

Shyly peeking through the open doors, I observed a bustle of boisterous activity. Like ants, a handful of energetic souls scurried about. Two "worker ants" struggled to push an uncooperative dolly holding the bulky net out to the middle of the floor.

Out of the corner of my eye, I spotted a slender girl with brown, shoulder-length hair walking toward me.

"I'm glad you could make it!" Sue greeted me. "Come on, let's go change."

When we returned, I stared in awe at the spectacle greeting my eyes. A haphazard-looking concoction of cables, poles and ropes tightly suspended the net about six feet off the floor. It seemed to stretch out forever.

We walked to the back of the line of people waiting to try the trapeze.

"When I was little," I confided to Sue, "my parents took me to the circus every year. I always wanted to be a flier. When I was eight, the ringmaster announced that the little boy in the flying act was six. I left that night practically in tears."

"Why?" Sue asked.

"Because I was already too old!"

My friend burst out laughing.

"Hey, it's not funny," I said. "If I was too old when I was eight, that makes me a relic at twenty-three!"

"Hi." A blond-haired man with a disarming smile walked up behind Sue and wrapped his arms around her waist. "Who's your friend?"

"Vickie, this is Alton. He's one of our catchers."

"Hello," I said, feeling shy, tongue-tied and out of place all at the same time.

Just then, another woman walked through the door and Alton glided away. Everyone seemed to know everyone else, but as fast as Sue introduced me, names scurried out of my mind.

From the buzz of voices, I picked up on some of the lingo. Two nets called "aprons" rose high in the air at either end of the main net, called the "bed." A rope ladder dangled down from the "pedestal," a small, wooden platform where three fliers presently stood.

Spellbound, I turned my attention to the flier in the middle—a man in his mid- to late-thirties with thinning blond hair. A white leotard and tights covered his muscular frame.

"That's Bob," Sue said. "He used to fly with Ringling."

"Really?" I watched him grab the "flybar" when it swung toward him. He jumped high in the air and swung away from the pedestal with the poise and grace of a professional.

A flier named Manny offered to help me off the pedestal when my turn came. My excitement mounted.

Sue stuck her hands into a tray full of white powder standing near the ladder and applied a generous coat of chalk. When she began her ascent, I "chalked up." After four or five swings, Sue let go of the flybar and bounced into the net, landing safely on her back.

My turn!

A shiver of apprehension took me by surprise, but I quickly brushed it aside. Weighing in at a trim 103 pounds, I easily scampered up the makeshift ladder, but once on the pedestal, my confidence wavered again.

"Come stand in the middle," Manny urged.

While keeping a white-knuckled death-grip on the side cable, I cautiously inched toward the center.

Manny crossed over from the other side and stood behind me. "I've got you," he said, putting an arm around my waist. "Now reach out with both hands and grab the bar when it swings toward you."

My mouth felt like someone had stuffed giant wads of cotton inside. When the bar swung up, I lunged for it, curling my fingers around the white tape.

Manny calmly lifted me up and let go. Immediately I found myself swinging away from him. All fear vanished as I tried to pump out with my legs at the far end of the swing like I'd seen others do. At the back of the swing, my legs naturally came forward when I arched my back.

After a few swings, Manny yelled, "Hep!" I let go of the bar at the crest of my swing and made a perfect touchdown on my back. Crawling to the side of the net, I grabbed hold and deftly rolled over the edge.

"What do you think?" Sue asked.

"I'm hooked!"

Before my next turn, I watched Alton climb a thick rope hand over hand until he reached the "catch trap" which hung down opposite the pedestal. It differed from the flybar in that thick padding wrapped around its shorter cables, extending a couple of feet up from the bar. Alton stretched an arm out, closing first one hand, then the other, around the bar. Next, he hooked his knees over the bar and pulled himself into a sitting position. After he pumped his legs back and forth to build momentum, he turned his head and looked inquiringly at Bob.

"I'll do a layout," Bob stated.

Alton dropped into his "catcher's lock." He placed both hands in the middle of the bar at the back of his swing, smoothly dropped backward and wrapped his legs around the padding. Bob performed a beautiful high back somersault. With perfect timing, he finished rotating just as Alton reached the peak of his swing. I heard the *Slap!* as their extended arms met and they swung out over the catch apron. On the return swing, Bob pushed off from Alton's hands, turned and grabbed the flybar for a flawless return to the pedestal.

On my next turn, Manny had me do a knee-hang. When I swung out, I pulled my knees over the bar. After clearing the pedestal at the back, I let go with my hands, stretched out and saw Alton sitting up-right on the catch trap.

Swinging away from him, I reached up for the bar, unhooked my knees when the momentum carried me back out and dropped into the net.

"That was fun!" I gasped.

Manny flashed me a smile. "You're ready to go to the catcher."

"Really?" I lost no time getting back in line.

"She's going to do a knee-hang," Manny yelled to Alton when my next turn came.

My cheeks felt flushed. Alton pumped up his swing and dropped into his catcher's lock. At the right moment, Manny let me off.

As if on automatic pilot, my body went through the same motions. When I reached out, I looked into Alton's sparkling blue eyes.

At the precise moment our wrists locked to-gether, I fell in love. Thus began my latest serious love affair—trapeze! As I soared through the air, I realized I had finally discovered what I had been searching for my whole life—the ultimate adrena-line rush. My activities of the past—skiing, climb-ing, skydiving, hang gliding—didn't even come close to the newfound thrill of flying trapeze.

The following weeks found me "hitting the bars" every Wednesday and Friday night, when the fliers had use of the gym.

Two months down the road I invited the trapeze crowd over for my specialty, homemade burritos.

When the doorbell rang that night, I came face to feet with three pairs of ratty-looking sneakers. Following the shoes and jeans down to the concrete, I discovered three familiar bodies straining to stay balanced on their hands. Seconds later, Bruce, Mark and Tony sprang to their feet.

While they marched through the door, a van pulled up and a young man with dark hair and a mustache emerged. When he walked toward me, my heart started pounding.

"Hello, Vickie."

"Hi, Gary. Come in," I managed to squeak, feeling like an awkward adolescent.

More people arrived and soon lively conversation and loud music filled the house. The rich aroma of spicy green chili wafted through the air. Finally I found myself spooning sauce and grated cheese into one last flour tortilla. Looking up, I handed it to the only person left in line—Gary.

"Is it OK if I sit in here?" he asked, pointing to the tiny counter and wooden stools.

I gulped. "That's fine . . . ah, mind if I join you?"

He smiled. "Sure!"

Gary and I talked while other fliers wandered in and out of the kitchen to refill their plates.

"I wanted to start swinging last spring," Gary explained. "After I finished playing racquetball one night, I walked past the gym and saw the trapeze. They'd just started to tear down. I was going to try it the next week, then I broke my leg."

"How did you do that?"

"Skiing. I fell and one of my bindings didn't release."

"Ouch!" I winced. "When did you finally get back to the Y?"

"The week before you started. It took my leg a long time to heal. How did you find out about trapeze?" Gary asked.

"Sue told me about it. It's been a dream come true. Ever since I can remember, I've wanted to do trapeze."

Gary cocked his head. "No kidding? Me too!"

Twenty minutes later Gary headed for the living room while I tidied up a bit. When I left the kitchen, I spotted him talking to Bob.

Gary smiled when I approached. "Everyone's invited over to swing on Bob's casting rig. He's setting it up tomorrow at a park north of here. He and his wife used to do an act on it in the circus."

"Really?" Wide-eyed, I turned to Bob. "I'll be there," I promised.

When Bob took his leave, the party gravitated toward the door until only one flier remained. Gary lingered a moment in the doorway. Then, to my surprise, he turned and put his arm around my shoulders. Looking up into his eyes, I melted into his kiss. Moments later he climbed into his van while my mind reeled.

When I arrived at the park the next morning, a group of familiar faces huddled around a chaotic assortment of gold pipes, cables, mats and duffel bags. When I walked over, Bob welcomed me and handed me a rag.

"Vickie, would you help Tony and Gary wipe off the rest of the pipes?"

Gary's smile assured me that we would see more of each other in the days to come. Soon another carload of fliers pulled up.

"You couldn't have picked a nicer day," I said to Bob. Nearby trees, limbs ablaze with flashy reds and yellows, had recently started to shed. Leaves crackled in the cool breeze when I stepped on them.

"Now listen up and I'll explain how to assemble the rig," Bob said.

Once we had the poles fitted together, he showed Tony and Gary how to hoist the rig up into the air.

"That went fast!" someone exclaimed.

Bob inspected all the cables. "When my wife and I were with the Shrine Circus, the two of us could put it up in twenty minutes flat. And it only took four prop-hands to carry it into the ring for us."

How exciting!

After Bob unfolded the mats, he grabbed the flybar—a short hop from the ground—and shoved it forward to get it swinging. Then he climbed the four steps to the pedestal. Reaching for the bar when it swung toward him, he took a few practice swings, turned at the far end and mounted the pedestal. Next, he reached up and pulled a cable that snaked through pulleys attached to the upper horizontal pipes. The end of the cable clipped onto a ring mounted on a rigid bar at the far end called the "catch."

All eyes focused on Bob as he did a straight jump across to the catch and sailed away on that bar. When he swung back he dropped to the ground.

"Who wants to take a swing?"

"I do," Gary said.

"Me too," I heard myself say.

A line formed behind us. Few fliers showed interest in attempting a trick to the catch, but Bob didn't have any trouble talking Gary and me into doing a simple hocks across. He told me how high to pump up the catch and how to judge the proper timing for takeoff.

I gripped the bar in the center and waited till I started back out on my second swing to pull both legs up to the bar—outside my hands. Just before the top of the swing, I hooked my knees, dropped backward, spun under the bar and grabbed the catch when it came toward me.

"Wow, it's so quick. I love it!"

One night after practice the following week, Gary and I joined the other fliers down at a nearby restaurant. In between ordering drinks and munchies, I caught snatches of Gary's discussion with Bob. The week before we had asked Bob if he knew how we could "break in" to the circus. As they talked Bob whipped out a small notebook and turned toward Gary. I leaned in.

"I can get both of you work for next season doing the casting act if you can learn all the tricks by Christmas."

Dumbstruck, Gary and I stared at each other. Without a moment's hesitation, we both said, "Sure!"

"When can we start practicing?" I asked.

Bob smiled. "How about tomorrow?"

◆—◆—◆—◆—◆—◆

Bob's casting rig nestled snugly between the ancient elm and the south fence of his modest backyard. Every weekend, plus Tuesday and Thursday afternoons after my last semester of classes at the University of Denver that November and December, Gary and I hit the bars under our trainer's supervision.

"Gary, you need to stop shoving the flybar out of Vickie's reach when you go across," Bob said one afternoon. "Try the passing leap again, and this time really concentrate on leaving a good bar."

I dusted myself off and followed Gary back up to the pedestal.

"Vickie, when you pop into the splits, point your toes. That looked sloppy."

After a few deep breaths, I pulled the cable to pump up the catch and moved to the center of the pedestal. This time I did a smooth splits across, swung back, let go, turned and for the first time found a flybar within reach. On my backswing, Gary let go of the catch, turned and grabbed the flybar. Side by side we made our first successful return to the pedestal.

Gary leaned over and planted a kiss on my lips. We had just successfully caught the last trick on Bob's list—three weeks ahead of his deadline. A thought teased my mind. *And they ran away and joined the circus and lived happily ever after. What more could I want out of life?*

* * *

Gary's face dropped. "Comedy? Me?"

After Christmas Bob had explained the stumbling bumbling clown character that Gary would portray. Quiet and shy like me, Gary seemed to want to run away from the circus about now. I felt very lucky because I would play the graceful showgirl—who looked none too graceful yet.

As the days crowded together, a gradual transformation took place. Gary's clown-self started rubbing off, adding a new dimension to his serious, no-nonsense personality. He might not have caught the subtle change—the unexpected smile or the silly grin that occasionally lit up his face—but I welcomed it.

Bob did a good job of selling two wannabe performers—sight unseen; talent questionable; circus history, nil. The last week in February he received a contract from a small show that played inside shopping malls throughout the midwest. April 10 through 14 we would perform in Mesquite, Texas; April 17 through 21 we would perform in Burlington, Iowa.

If the owner liked the act, he'd hire us for the whole season.

Gary and I eagerly accepted.

CHAPTER FOUR

Circus Life

"What a huge mall!" I said. "Nothing in Denver comes close to matching this."

"It's a great setting for a circus," Gary added.

Good grief. We're performing here in less than twenty-four hours! What in the world have I gotten myself into?

Gary and I scouted out the show area while Bob kept a lookout for the owners. Almost every store we passed contained big, bold placards screaming, "Sale!" With a start I realized that I would have the entire week to check them out. The thought scared me. Three half-hour shows a day would leave me with way too much free time to spend money!

On the third floor we found a huge expanse of empty marble floor space in front of carpeted oversized bleachers, deserted except for a couple of weary shoppers resting their feet. When we headed back out to the parking lot, we spotted two trailers.

We chatted with Earl and Lou, the owners of the show, while their teenage son, Tim, unhitched their trailer in the parking lot. This seemed as odd as our future task of setting up a casting rig inside a mall 912 miles from home.

Once the stores closed, Gary, Bob and I started hauling stuff inside. The two men struggled with the cumbersome mats. I slung the not-so-light duffel bag over my shoulder, grabbed the flybar and we set off. Five exhausting trips later, we watched Tim drive his folks' truck toward us.

I gasped. "We could have driven right in? Do we ever have a lot to learn!"

Bob helped Gary and me set up the rig while Tim unloaded the show equipment. We met the juggler and his wife that night, but the other act didn't pull in until morning.

Thinking about the next day gave me a bad case of "night before the opening show" jitters. *Why did I want to do this in the first place?* As a kid, I died a thousand deaths when forced to stand in front of the class to read a book report. But somehow running away to join the circus had seemed different.

Maybe wanderlust ran in my family. I remembered my father's marvelous stories about the days, long before my birth, when he'd traveled around the country booking his own shows. His passion: magic! I recalled browsing through his scrapbooks reading neatly folded newspaper clippings from all over the country.

That night, lying on the carpeted floor of Gary's van a mere ten inches away from him, I felt a great wall between us. We'd broken up two months earlier when another woman entered the picture. After removing my shoes, I kept my jeans and T-shirt on as did my ex-boyfriend. I tried to keep my mind off the heat, the cramped sleeping quarters and the creeping loneliness by focusing on tomorrow. Why worry later when I could start now?

The next morning I awoke with a start and immediately peered at my watch. In precisely two hours and twelve minutes the show would go on. How could Gary sleep so peacefully? Didn't he know he should wake up and begin worrying at once?

Quietly, I slipped out and marched inside to the food court where I ran into Earl and Lou. They looked so different! Earl, decked out in a pale blue dress shirt, black tails and elegant top hat, looked every bit the circus ringmaster. A bright red dress with matching sequined jacket replaced Lou's faded jumper of the night before.

* * *

Circus performers typically wear robes over their costumes while waiting to perform, but I felt self-conscious wearing a bathrobe in a mall. Of course, the rhinestone-trimmed outfit underneath didn't help matters either. Spirited circus tunes drifted through the air long before we reached the show. Rounding a corner to head backstage, I marveled at the sight.

When we'd left last night, Tim hadn't finished setting everything up. Now, sparkly silver curtains graced both sides of the bandstand. An ornate sign read, "TNT and Royal Olympic Circus." Lou made beautiful music on a small organ while Tim beat out rhythm on the drums.

Unlike most American circuses, this show copied the European format: one ring, one act performed at a time. No three-ring circus here!

Beside the ring there were two long white poles with assorted hardware attached to the top and bottom—a perch! *The other act made it!* Backstage I could see three new adult faces, a toddler and the back of a baby stroller.

Even though the free entertainment would not begin for another twenty minutes, the bleachers had already started to fill with shoppers. Mothers with babies, teenagers and children in a wide variety of shapes and sizes waited expectantly—for us. *They're waiting for us!*

"Are you the same person we met last night?" I asked the tall pink and purple clown with exquisitely painted face and bright sparkly hat who sat tapping the drums.

"The one and only!" Tim replied with a grin.

While Gary started warming up, I talked with the new couple, Carol and Carlos, and with Brenda— the slender young woman they had hired to do the perch act with Carlos.

The juggler's wife looked bored to the point of tears. Here I was, so nervous I thought surely I'd explode any second, and she couldn't stop yawning!

All too soon the music ended. Amidst drumrolls and a giant poof of smoke from a "flashpot"—a device detonated by a switch Tim triggered—Earl made his grand entrance.

"Ladies and gentlemen! Children of all ages!" His announcement drew a few stragglers as the fast-paced juggler and his lethargic assistant opened the show.

I pulled a small baggie out of the roomy pocket in my new "bathrobe made for wearing over a circus costume in a shopping mall," crumbled resin into my palms and handed the bag to Gary.

After their finale, Earl announced the "Carlos Duo." The knot in my stomach grew when Brenda and Carlos stepped through the curtains. Brenda wore a white leotard adorned with red rhinestones that glittered under the bright lights. Fishnet stockings and gold high heels completed the picture.

From backstage I watched her gracefully shinning the pole balanced on Carlos' shoulders, but then I broke into heavy-duty worrying and ignored the rest of the act. After the pair took their final bows, Tim burst through the curtains to begin his clown gag.

Self-consciously, I walked out with Gary to set the mats under the rig and to put our other props in place. A sweet little blond-haired, blue-eyed doll escaped her mother's grasp and toddled over to me, her mother two steps behind. Watching them walk back to their seats, I smiled. She could have passed for one of the toddlers that comprised our first audience in Bob's backyard. Recalling the excitement we'd felt performing for the first time before those three kids, a light flashed on. *We can do this!*

The audience howled when Tim delivered the punch line of his washerwoman gag. He bounded backstage out of breath and flashed us a big grin. "Break a leg!"

"And now," Earl's voice boomed over the mike, "all the way from Denver, Colorado, prepare yourselves for rib-tickling antics on the low-flying trapeze with Grinn and Barrett!"

With that, we sailed out and began one of the most exciting careers of our lives. The act unfolded like clockwork. What beautiful, noisy children! By the time Gary's clown pants fell down, revealing his matching turquoise costume beneath, the adults laughed out loud along with the kids. We finished to thunderous applause and breezed back through the curtains.

"We did it!" I said.

"What a great audience!" Gary added.

When I drifted off to sleep that night, children's laughter pealed through my dreams.

At the end of the two week engagement, Earl offered us a contract for the rest of the season, which would start in five weeks. We eagerly accepted.

That first year brought many new experiences. Gary and I traveled across the country together, hauling the rig for the act inside Gary's van. On one trip—the longest of the entire season—we became physically intimate.

With the change in our relationship the loneliness I had felt all summer seemed to melt away. Everything seemed better: the music seemed livelier, the lights cheerier, the audience more responsive.

The next three weeks passed quickly, and before I knew it, the tour had brought us to a mall in Denver.

All summer I had looked forward to playing my home town again, but this welcome new romantic development might cause waves—something I tried to avoid at all costs. My parents, out of the country when we'd played Denver in June, would watch us perform for the first time tomorrow night.

"Are you going to tell your mom?" Gary asked as we neared the city limits.

I sighed. "If she asks, I'll tell her the truth, but I'm not going to volunteer anything. I already know what she'll say. She'll think it's wrong. She won't approve of us living together in a million years. . . . You don't think she'll ask, do you?" I looked out the window and squirmed.

She asked. In fact, the unwanted conversation occurred the very next day. On a missed passing leap during the first show, I broke my arm and needed to ask Mom for a ride back from the doctor's office. The afternoon show would start before I could get plastered—so to speak—and Gary had temporarily become a member of the perch act (renamed The Carlos Trio). Four nights earlier Carlos had broken his leg—on our rig, no less—and he needed an assistant to help him in his act.

As it turned out, Mom already knew what I hadn't wanted to tell her. At the time, I couldn't understand why she thought it was wrong for Gary and me to live together. After all, everybody was doing it.

Since I could not swing with a cast on my arm, Bob came up with a backup plan for Gary and me. We kept all of Gary's pratfalls in, but I stayed off the bars. Despite our initial apprehension, the remaining six weeks of the "Plan B" tour went over well with "children of all ages."

The last week of performances brought many offers. We signed a contract with Earl agreeing to perform a unique balancing act not yet put together, doing tricks not yet learned, with props not yet constructed, wearing wardrobes not yet designed!

We also signed a contract with an agent we had acquired over the summer to do a two-week Christmas tour in the midwest.

I took Carol and Carlos up on their offer to perform the perch act with Carlos for a two-week "spot date" they had booked months ago for February. Brenda had made other plans, and they desperately needed a warm body—even an untrained one—to fulfill their contract. The doctor would remove my cast over Christmas, so I jumped at the opportunity to perform. I had as much experience doing perch as I had with hand balancing—none whatsoever—but this didn't seem to bother anyone.

Tim asked Gary and me if we would perform in a sideshow that he was booking separately at some of the malls lined up for next season. He wanted me to curl up inside a wooden box while he stuck swords through it. Gary turned him down. My response? "Sure!"

Tim also needed a fire-eater—again, no experience necessary.

"Sure!"

Our second year proved interesting. In addition to designing and learning the balancing act, "Annie and Her Soldier," Gary bought a thirty-five foot Greyhound bus. We removed all the seats, decorated it in "early temporary" and hit the road running in April.

By mid-season, Gary and I had decided to go with a Shrine circus the following year. We weren't any closer to having a trapeze rigging built or a flying act prepared, so we opted to do the casting act and the balancing act for one more season. To get work with that show, our agent told us that we needed to have a third act, so we wound up buying Carol and Carlos' perch. Astonished, we wondered once again how many other performers got work for an act before they actually had the act!

Our season with George Carden's Shrine Circus stretched into two, with a wedding thrown in the middle—ours! Until she got that phone call from Canada, Mom probably thought she'd heard it all.

"Hello, Mom . . . yes, your schedule is right. We're in Sioux St. Marie, Canada. . . . Say, I have some exciting news. Are you sitting down? Gary and I are getting married! Oh, uh . . . when?"

I took a deep breath. "Next Friday when we play Ottawa. In the center ring. During intermission. . . . Hello?"

In the end, we waited and married two months later in my parents' backyard. July 10 was a bright and clear day, and crystal blue skies graced the 5 p.m. ceremony. Gary's family drove out from Delaware and assorted aunts and uncles on my side materialized from California and Missouri. Much to my mother's relief, nothing out of the ordinary happened. None of my skydiver friends "dropped in," no lions or tigers or elephants paraded by and we did not stand high above the ground on a trapeze pedestal to take our vows before swinging off into the sunset. The yard wasn't big enough. I checked.

CHAPTER FIVE

The Flying Act

━━◆━◆━◆━◆━◆━━

A shiver of excitement raced through my body. *Today's the day!*

"Hang on, we're almost there," I murmured to the twelve pounds of wiggling fluff that tried to squirm out of my lap. I turned to Gary. "You know, we haven't had Fliffus very long, but it's hard to imagine life on the road without her."

Gary reached over to scratch her ears and got treated to a handful of enthusiastic doggie kisses.

For years, I had hounded Gary about getting a dog. Last spring, he surprised me by consenting, so I acted fast. Never mind that we were midway through a two-week engagement at an amusement park in Pittsburgh—my husband had said "yes!"

Two days later, an ad in a local paper prompted a telephone call. After the 4:00 show, Gary and I took a long drive through the hilly, green countryside. We came back with a six-week-old bundle of yapping, slurping, tail-thumping energy that insisted on sleeping with us and not in a cardboard box, thank you very much. In practically no time at all, she had us trained.

I held on to Fliffus while Gary drove. *If it feels right today, I'll go for it.* We turned off a two-lane highway just outside the small town of Haines City. Our friend, John, a former flier with Ringling, owned a ranch-style house—the second one on the right. We pulled into his driveway and Snoopy, John's trusty watch-beagle, raced out of his lonely doghouse, hoping we'd brought his playmate. When I opened my door, a blur of curly white fur flew past to greet her buddy.

Every morning when we arrived for practice, the sight practically took my breath away. Our flying rig occupied ideal winter quarters—no doubt about it. John graciously allowed us to play in his backyard—a beautiful piece of property, which was bordered on three sides by groves of orange trees. It contained ample room for setting up an entire circus.

Between his trampoline and low-wire stood our new flying rig. Sunlight glinted off shiny aluminum uprights that rose some thirty-five feet in the air. We had taken last summer off to build this beauty and to start working up an act.

Our brand-new three-ply net stretched between the uprights. I spent many a tedious afternoon the previous summer weaving rubber-banded bundles of horizontal ropes through rubber-banded bundles of vertical ropes. With my nimble fingers, I could weave circles around Gary.

Building our rig had worked out just like our last major project—a robin's-egg blue kitchen countertop for the bus: Gary supplied the know-how and I helped with the grunt work. Offhand, I could think of nothing that my husband could not build, construct, design or fix.

The custom-made ladder leading up to the pedestal beckoned to us long before we finished our strenuous warm-up routine.

"Gary, I did twenty-two pull-ups!" I gasped after I dropped to the ground. "Yesterday, my limit was twenty-one. When we started last month, I could only do twelve."

"Working out twice a day is making a big difference," Gary said from his perch on the low wire pedestal. "We're both swinging higher too. At the rate we're going, by the time we leave for Denver, we might have all the tricks down. Your two-and-a-half is almost there and I'm close to catching my fliffus—"

Upon hearing her name, our poodle cocked her head to one side and gave Gary an adoring "what do you want, Master?" look, not realizing that he spoke of the half-twisting double somersault after which we'd named her. We both laughed.

Gary left the safety of the pedestal. I watched each slow, deliberate step on the slender strand until he reached the other side.

"I still haven't made it all the way across," I grumbled.

From six feet up, Gary smiled. "It's a good thing we don't do high-wire."

"You can say that again! Give me trapeze any day. I don't even like to watch high-wire—especially after what happened in Brownsville." I shuddered, thinking back to that terrible day.

While we had waited to go on, we witnessed the two women in the wire act fall—nearly thirty feet—to the hard concrete floor. We stood backstage in shock when the owner rushed over to tell us to go on—*now*. Neither of us performed very well, but no one paid us much heed until the paramedics arrived and carried the two women off on stretchers. Surprisingly, we saw both women up and walking around the next day.

"At least with trapeze," I said, "no matter how much I mess up on a trick, I have a nice cushy net to land in."

Just then, a truck pulled up and a stocky man with thick, blond hair stepped out.

"Hi, Mark!" we both yelled.

He flashed us both a smile and then turned to me. "Are you ready, Vickie?"

My pulse quickened. I tried to smile back. "Possibly, it depends on how I do in the belt."

Ever since I'd put on a spotting belt and tried a one-and-a-half at the YMCA, I'd set my sights on the heart-stopping thrill of mastering the two-and-a-half. For the two-and-a-half, the flier breaks out of a "legs trick"—a trick where he or she is caught in an upside down position by the legs instead of the wrists. On a miss, I needed to react instantly—duck my head and twist to my back—to land safely in the net. Would I?

We climbed up to the pedestal. From our lofty perch, I saw Bob's car chugging down the dirt road.

My two-and-a-half required team effort. For an entire month now, Mark had driven over every morning to play catcher for us and to call me on my break-out. Bob called my timing for takeoff and manned the ropes on the spotting belt. Gary handed me the flybar. John had watched us practice yesterday and told me something that I already suspected.

"You have the trick, Vickie. It's time to take the belt off. Now it's just slowing you down."

His words, etched in my mind, had spoken confidence to my heart last night. But now, as the moment of truth approached, doubt and fear took over.

By the time we finished doing our warm-up swings, I had calmed myself down. Hand over hand, Mark pulled himself up to the catch. I finished buckling the padded belt around my waist and Gary snapped the ropes through the rings on either side of the belt. Bob donned a pair of leather gloves, picked up the ropes that threaded through pulleys high above my head and nodded.

"I'm ready when you are," he yelled.

I pulled myself up onto the rise board. "OK, Mark."

Mark pumped up his swing and dropped into his catcher's lock. Gary swung the bar up to me.

I took a deep breath. *Concentrate, Vickie.*

"Hep!" Bob yelled.

Like all other mornings, I leaped up, drove my legs behind me and swung out. At the far end of my second swing, I rose in the air, let go of the bar and tucked into a tight ball. Mark's "Hep!" called me out. When I straightened, I felt his firm grip around my legs. I stretched out full, but as usual, the belt slowed me down and killed the swing.

"Good one!" Bob said.

I dropped into the net on my back with a smile firmly attached. *One down.* Unhooking the ropes, I carried them back up. Gary clipped them onto either side of the pedestal to keep them out of his way while he took a turn. I watched his first attempt at catching a fliffus. He came close. Bob gave him some pointers.

I clipped the safety ropes back onto the belt. My second and third attempts also resulted in good, solid catches.

"Looking good," Bob said.

I smiled. Half walking, half bouncing across the net, I confidently scampered back up the ladder. Before I could talk myself out of it, I clipped the ropes onto either side of the pedestal and yelled to Mark, "Two-and-a-half!"

Go for it.

"Do everything the same way you've been doing it," Gary said. "You'll do fine."

I knew he meant to reassure me, but I caught the troubled look in his eye and picked up on the tense tone of voice. As I pulled myself onto the rise board, every eye turned toward me. I wondered if anyone else heard the deafening thump of my heart.

Relax, you have it down.

I nodded to Gary. He swung the flybar up to me. Taking a deep breath, I watched Mark drop into his catcher's lock. Bob yelled, "Hep!" I sprang into the air, pumped up my swing at the front, held my legs behind me until the swing's momentum shot me *up up up* behind the pedestal. *Now keep your head up.* I swung back out.

"Hep!"

Forcing my legs behind me, I let go of the bar and sailed up, rotating in a tight tucked position. *Just do it the same.*

"Hep!"

Break out.

I began to straighten when I felt Mark's reassuring grasp. We swung away.

I did it!

We swung out over the catch apron. I could almost touch the even squares in front of my outstretched hands. On the return swing, I twisted my upper body around, grabbed the flybar that magically appeared in front of my eyes and mounted the pedestal. *Yes!* Gary leaned over and gave me a kiss. "Congratulations!"

"You have it!" Bob yelled.

Another flawless two-and-a-half soon followed. After my third secure catch, I dropped to the net, wanting desperately to take a break, but wanting even more to get it over with. The big "what if" still hung heavy in the air. *What if I land wrong? Eventually I'll miss—what then? Will I do it right? Will I twist out OK?* Sensing my concern, Gary told me to come up and try one more.

Suddenly, a gust of wind appeared from nowhere. *Should I wait? No, I don't want to go through this again.* The blast of air disappeared, so I climbed back up the ladder, pulled my weary body up onto the rise board and nodded to Mark.

A stray thought popped into my mind. *Be careful.* Typical parting advice from my mother. *Be careful.* Words that never seemed to change over the years. *Be careful.*

I watched Mark drop into his lock, waited for Bob to call me off the pedestal.

"Hep!"

Be careful.

Leaving the security of terra firma behind, my body automatically repeated its previous performance. Good, high swing . . . good timing . . . good tuck . . . be careful. But suddenly something went terribly wrong. The catcher pushed me away. His rejection sent me spinning down, plummeting through space. Down. Down. Down. My mind kicked into red alert mode. *Twist to your back, Vickie. Duck your head, Vickie. Be careful, Vickie.*

My mind went to work. With the control and grace of a cat tossed in midair, my body twisted. My head pulled forward.

Will I make it in time? I touched down on my back—a perfect, controlled landing. The springy net gently cradled my body. I sank down deep.

The net playfully bounced me high in the air. Safe on my back, I flung my arms out to maintain control. Coming to a stop, I smiled at the heavens above. I smiled at the powder-puff clouds dotting the sky. I smiled up at Gary smiling down at me. Warmth returned to my cheeks.

◆━◆━◆━◆━◆

Winter passed quickly—our thoughts caught up in a whirlwind of carefully mapped out plans and goals for the new act. Two days before we tore down and loaded up for our migration back to Denver, Gary and I caught our first successful passing leap. At this point, Gary had begun to catch his fliffus, a half-twisting double to a stick held in the catcher's hands—always a crowd-pleaser. We just knew that we'd have a first-rate flying act by next fall. No doubt about it!

CHAPTER SIX

Lost in Midair

◆▬◆▬◆▬◆▬◆

The annoying whine of an engine broke into my dreams, pulling me into a state of semiconsciousness. The sweet aroma of freshly cut grass wafted through an open window at the back of the bus. I yawned, stretched, then tried to picture my surroundings. On the road, we played many one-day-stands and parked anywhere from bustling truck stops along the interstate to quiet, out of the way campgrounds, to coliseum parking lots where we frequently awoke to the bellow of hungry tigers.

Let's see . . . we're in Denver. The rig is straight ahead of us in Bruce's backyard . . . the mountains are behind us.

I reached over and pulled aside the quilted curtain. A crisp, spring morning, complete with a cloudless, royal-blue backdrop so typical of Colorado, met my bleary-eyed gaze. Another calm, sunshiny day beckoned. Another perfect day for flying.

It's really happening—we're finally getting the act together! People aren't supposed to be this happy when they grow up, are they?

A shiver of excitement jerked me awake. We had taken the entire summer off and had our very own flying rig set up just outside. Life couldn't get any better.

My mind drifted back to the spot date in Des Moines last week. Our agent had come through with work for us along the "let's get out of Florida before summer" escape route. What a great show too. During the casting act the kids laughed really hard and we got a standing ovation!

I recalled a fellow performer's unusual remarks about working concessions there. With a hint of annoyance in his voice, Dino had said, "I might as well take a break during 'Grinn and Barrett.' The kids all give you their undivided attention." Little did we know when we tore down that I would never again get to make children laugh when the circus came to town.

According to our self-imposed schedule, we drove straight through after the last show on Sunday, parked behind Bruce's house and got the rig up the very next day. But we hadn't planned on Bruce pulling a shoulder muscle the Wednesday before and we hadn't planned on having to scrounge around for another catcher. Not a major problem, but a problem nonetheless.

I glanced over at the stationary form curled up beside me. My husband wouldn't crack an eyelid for at least an hour.

Meanwhile, a more urgent concern gnawed at my stomach. *What sounds good this morning? Waffles? Hash browns? I've got it—apple pancakes! Yes, it definitely feels like an apple pancake morning.* Having settled the matter, I pulled the covers back and quietly slipped out of bed.

While wolfing down seconds, I couldn't tear my eyes off the paperback clutched in my hand. The true story of a seventeen-year-old girl who broke her neck diving into shallow water—she had hit her head on the bottom. I had sobbed my way through Joni's book twice now. She had become a quadriplegic, sentenced to spend the rest of her life in a wheelchair—in my eyes, a fate worse than death itself. Goosebumps shivered down my arms.

Just then, Gary lumbered toward the kitchen.

"There's a little batter left," I called out. "Would you like some pancakes?"

A grunt and a blank stare greeted me.

"Oh, sorry. I keep forgetting that you don't like to eat right away." How someone could not want breakfast immediately after waking up remained a mystery to me. With all the energy I expended each day, I seemed to have food on my mind constantly. Once, during a show up in Canada, I even debated on what to fix for dinner while balanced atop the perch—some twenty feet above a very unforgiving concrete floor. I believe tacos won out that night.

I brought my empty plate over to the sink and gave the lone avocado a squeeze. *Good, it's finally ripe. I can fix guacamole for lunch.* Sometimes whole meals revolved around the ripeness of the avocados I bought. Fortunately, I loved to cook every bit as much as I loved to eat.

After washing the dishes, I picked up my hand guards and wandered outside. Twenty minutes later Gary joined me in the backyard. We took turns bouncing on Bruce's trampoline. I kept visualizing my two-and-a-half over and over in my mind.

After three solid days of missing the trick, it had begun to spook me. *Why am I allowing this silly trick to scare me so much? Why can't I catch it?* I'd made good solid catches down in Florida for over a month now. What happened?

With Gary temporarily filling in for me as catcher, I thought I'd come close to catching it yesterday. But when we played the tape again last night, we decided that I needed to break out sooner. And swing higher. And tuck tighter. The "ands" seemed to stretch on indefinitely.

I don't want to go back to using the spotting belt. Besides, we don't have the pulleys and ropes rigged up yet and we don't have anyone to spot me. I just need to concentrate harder. Maybe today will be my lucky day.

"Do you have the rosin bag?" Gary asked as he started up the ladder.

"Yup."

A few minutes later, we both took a warm-up swing and my silly fears began to disappear. *I haven't lost the trick. I know I haven't—I bet I catch it today. I have a feeling this will be one day I'll long remember.*

Standing on the pedestal twenty-eight feet above the ground gave us a great view of Bruce's quiet neighborhood as well as the majestic Rockies off in the distance. The sight of Mount Evans, still covered with snow, practically took my breath away. I savored the change of scenery from the constant parade of citrus trees down in Florida and looked forward to spending the whole summer flying.

I drank in the woodsy fragrance of an Australian pine growing directly behind the pedestal and watched a robin scold me every time she lined up an approach pattern to return to her nest. The delightful scent of vanilla emanated from delicate white clematis blossoms covering a fence that separated Bruce's yard from his neighbor's. Beyond the fence, a flamboyant splash of orange and black poppies caught my eye. Springtime in the Rockies—what a treat.

Gary took a couple more swings, then dropped into the net and climbed up to the catch. I felt certain that we would connect this time on my two-and-a-half. Adrenaline flowed through my body when I leaped off the pedestal, sure of success.

Nail it this time. You can do it. Take it away.

Seconds later, I lay uneasily in the net. What had I hit?

"Are you OK?"

"I'm not sure." Gary lowered himself hand over hand down the thick rope hanging next to the catch. I saw the pain in his eyes. He walked toward the bus, gingerly touching his face. I somberly followed. My knee must have caught him in the jaw when I broke out.

Gary carefully moved his mouth around. His fears that I dislocated his jaw proved wrong, but I still felt close to tears. *How could I have made such a stupid mistake?*

Twenty minutes later, we both returned to "the scene of the crime." I made my way back up the ladder to the pedestal while Gary returned to the catch.

"Try breaking out sooner," Gary yelled.

"OK."

I bent down and grabbed our eight-foot-long aluminum hook, wrapped my body securely around a pedestal upright, leaned way out and snagged the flybar. After inching it close enough, I caught the bar with the short stainless-steel hook tied to the pedestal. Then I replaced the long hook.

I sure hope we find someone that can practice with us during the day. This is getting to be a pain.

Next, I pulled the short hook toward me to release the flybar and moved to the center of the pedestal. Grabbing the upright to my left, I reached my other hand out for the bar when it swung close enough. I lifted it up one more time, let go and hopped up three feet higher onto the rise board. The next time the bar swung into reach, I stooped down to grab it and nodded at Gary. He dropped into his catcher's lock.

"Hep!"

I sprang into the air and curled my other hand around the bar. Then, as if watching a playback of my performance, I visualized freezing each frame where we would later stop the tape to observe my first successful catch to Gary. *Freeze*—leaping up, driving my legs behind me. *Freeze*—pumping out at the front of the swing. *Freeze*—shooting up high over the pedestal. *Freeze*—beating back hard with my legs. *Freeze*—letting go of the bar. My body rises in the air as I pull into a good tight tuck. *Freeze*—releasing my tuck . . . too late. *Abort trick!*

My God—what's wrong? Where am I?

My body does not twist out of the somersault. I lose control. My brain cannot sense my body's relationship to the net. For the briefest fraction of a second, I hesitate. I do not duck my head. My body seems to hang suspended in midair like a cartoon character before he realizes that he's just run off the edge of a cliff.

What happened next would change the course of my life forever. No one could alter the real life drama that played out before my eyes. No one on earth could erase this tape. No one.

I catch a glimpse of the net rushing up to embrace my body as I plunge down. Head first, I awkwardly hit the soft net. The forgiving net. The net that I personally spent countless hours weaving. My head sinks down, down, down. The net accommodates, gently caressing my topsy-turvy form.

But this time when I reach bottom, the net reveals a new side. Flashes a hidden secret. Flaunts its bottom line. Like an undertow just beneath the surface, hidden, yet deadly. When the net abruptly stops, it takes control. Catches me unawares on its rebound. Inflicts pressure on my neck. Forces my head back. Catapults me like a yo-yo. Flings my disheveled body upward.

Sproiiing.

From somewhere deep inside, I feel like a coiled spring has snapped. I gently bounce when I hit the net for the second time and come to rest on my right side. A soft breeze soothes my face.

Something is terribly wrong.

Warm sunshine continues to smile down on me, but my whole body tingles. I hear a buzzing noise in my head. Was it coming from inside me? I stare at my limbs sprawled out in disarray.

Why can't I feel anything?

A finch lands on the ridge rope not two feet from my face and sweetly chirps.

A heavy weight restrains me. Prevents me from moving. Like someone has tied me down with ropes—but I see no rope. I see nothing but crumpled up arms and legs. I stare at my limp left hand, resting not ten inches from my face. My mind sends out an urgent message.

Move, fingers!

Nothing happens.

Move, arm!

Again, nothing.

My horror mounts. I stare at my legs and feet, concentrating as hard as I can. Still nothing, not even a flicker. My body remains as lifeless as a corpse, as numb as my mouth after a shot of novocaine.

This is what happened to Joni!

Panic bubbles to the surface. I try to turn my neck.

My head moves! Thank God something *moves.*

A voice reaches into my spinning thoughts. I hear anguish that I've never heard before.

"Vickie—you landed on your head!"

My mouth opens. In a pitiful, trembling voice I squeak, "I can't move. I can't move. I can't move. Just like Joni, I can't move."

"Lie still," the powerful voice from above commands. *He knows what to do. He'll get help. He'll call 911.*

My mind flits around. Disconnected thoughts invade and recede. *When Joni hit her head, she didn't know what she'd done. She thought the numbness would wear off. I know better. I know what happened to me. I broke my neck—like that guy with Ringling who broke his neck doing a three-and-a-half. But he recovered. He's flying again. I'll recover. I'll fly again. If he could get better, I can too. Besides, we already signed a contract for next year. We can't break our contract. I'll get better, I just know I will.*

CHAPTER SEVEN

Room Number Six

◆─◆─◆─◆─◆─◆

The insistent shrill of a siren could be heard long before the shiny red fire truck screeched to a halt. Half a dozen big burly men streamed out. Gary spoke with them briefly, then they all headed toward me.

The squeal of tires and the slam of a car door signaled Bruce's timely arrival.

"Thanks for coming home from work," Gary said when our friend rounded the corner of the house. Clad in a suit and tie, Bruce looked about as out of place as the firemen who now had me surrounded.

"Hello."

I looked down and saw a shock of bright orange hair framing a round freckled face.

"Ma'am, can you breathe OK?"

"Yes."

"We're going to hold this under you while your husband and his friend lower the net."

Bruce and Gary each manned one of the blocks and pulleys while the firemen held up a board directly under the net to support my weight. The colossal net lowered to the ground inch by inch.

Just then a lone cloud skittered directly overhead, shrouding the sun's warmth. A chill crept down my spine. *What have I done? Why didn't I duck my head?*

At last I lay on the ground. Outside the fence stood an assortment of kids who had stopped to stare. I felt naked under their scrutiny.

An ambulance arrived and two new faces swam into focus. Many hands gently transferred my limp frame onto the cart they'd brought, taking great care to keep my neck immobilized. I wondered how long it would take me to recover; how long it would be before I could climb back up to the pedestal and take a swing. After the paramedics strapped me securely in place, they wheeled me out to the street.

"I'll follow in the car," Gary said.

Moments later, the mournful wail of the siren accompanied me to the hospital. My mistake continued to haunt me.

The rocking motion of the ambulance stopped and the shriek of the siren cut off abruptly, interrupting my thoughts. The back doors flew open and trained hands efficiently pulled the cart out and guided it toward two large blue doors. Somewhere close by I heard the shrill caw of a grackle.

The sweet perfume of spring flowers filled the air. Then the gaping doors opened and the emergency room swallowed me.

Once we were inside, the metal doors clanged shut, putting an end to life as I knew it. I found myself in a tiny cubicle where a new set of strangers transferred me onto a table and cut my Carden Circus T-shirt off of me. A small man with intense grey eyes asked me questions while he poked me with pins. I tried to pay attention but my thoughts continued to assault me. *You know how to twist out of a two-and-a-half. What went wrong?*

"Can you feel this?"

"Ah . . . no."

"How about this?"

"No." With each "no," my terror mounted.

I finally scored an "ouch!" when the man jabbed my upper arm. After he finished, another white-coated professional wheeled me down the hall. Gary caught up with us.

"Where are you taking her?" he asked.

"X-ray," she said. "You'll have to wait outside."

After a barrage of x-rays were taken, Gary accompanied us to another small room.

"You need to leave, sir," a gruff voice stated. "Vickie, you dislocated your spinal cord," the voice continued. "We need to get it realigned. To do this, we will keep your head immobilized with tongs. . . ." The nameless, faceless voice kept talking, but my mind wandered back to the trapeze.

Why did I land wrong? What happened?

63

"Screwed directly into your skull."

I gasped. "What?"

I heard no answer, but I saw someone to my left, felt pressure by my ear and heard the loud whine of a drill. Fading in and out of consciousness, I didn't remember much else until Gary came back in. He squeezed my hand to reassure me. I couldn't feel it. Everywhere I looked, invading lights glared, tense faces stared. Strange words ricocheted off the walls.

"Twelve pounds of traction . . ."

"Stryker frame . . ."

What language do these white-coated strangers speak?

Once they finished poking, drilling and grilling me, two of them took me for a ride. While we waited for the elevator, a stern, craggy-faced man introduced himself to Gary and insisted that my husband follow him. Gary's sudden departure squeezed bands of terror around my racing heart.

The elevator ride seemed to take forever. Finally the shiny silver doors slid open and my captors navigated cart and victim down another hallway. When we stopped, I caught the ominous words on the large wooden doors before they sprang open: Intensive Care Unit.

I was wheeled into a tiny room and abandoned. I heard the hollow footsteps of the two orderlies retreating. My gaze darted around the room as if looking for an escape route. Out of the corner of my eye I could see part of a narrow window beyond the foot of the bed and a television set mounted near the ceiling which I could not turn my head to watch. At least lights didn't glare at me: pain seemed to follow close on the heels of bright lights.

Shortly, a friendly face appeared. Compassionate eyes looked into mine. "Vickie, I need to insert this tube down your nose to suction out your stomach. I'll go real slow—"

Just then, Gary walked into the room. Relief washed over me. *Thank God he's back.*

"Hi, I'm Laura. I'm Vickie's nurse today. I was just explaining this procedure. . . ."

Gary held my limp hand while Laura guided the fat rubber tube down my right nostril. Tears welled up in my eyes. Finally the torture ended and she withdrew the tube. She promised to get me something for the pain I'd started to feel in my neck and left the room as quietly as she'd entered.

Gary began to pace back and forth as he told me what the doctors had said. My befuddled mind could not absorb the information he had just received. *Permanent quadriplegia? As in "forever and ever"?* I could not allow myself to think such a thing lest my mind shatter into a million tiny pieces.

Gary scowled. "The doctor said nothing would ever change."

"Well, who is he to play God?" I said. "Remember that guy who broke his neck on Ringling? Didn't we read in *Circus Report* that his family went back to Chile and he recovered?"

"Yes," Gary said. "He's flying again. You'll get better too. We'll beat this thing, Vickie, I know we will."

"If I work at it real hard, I bet I can walk out of this hospital. I'll show that doctor a thing or two. In fact, when we book our flying act here in Denver, I'll send him tickets to the show." The very thought brought a smile to my face.

At that moment my nurse returned. "This should help." Laura fiddled with the IV tube in my wrist. She then explained how and why she needed to turn me. Something about preventing pressure sores. She attached some sort of cover and bedding over the top of me that had a small opening for my face, and flipped the whole bed upside down. Because the ill-fitting cutout put unbearable pressure on my jaw, Gary sat on the floor for the next two hours supporting my chin in his cupped hands.

I stared at those hands as they helped ease my pain. Kind hands—that had first held mine six years ago. Calloused hands—from gripping the flybar during daily practice sessions. Gentle hands—wrapped around me when we went to sleep each night. Bandaged hands—from two new blisters. Just yesterday? Yesterday seemed like a lifetime ago.

The drugs kicked in and I drifted away.

An announcement booms over the mike: "Ladies and gentlemen, the act you've all been waiting for!" After styling to a packed house, we remove our capes and ascend the ladder. I will perform my two-and-a-half. Taking my cues from the catcher, I leap high in the air. Suddenly, I'm falling.

I awakened with a start, facing the ceiling. When I saw the stained acoustical squares above my head, memory returned and the reality of quadriplegia slammed home.

Gary sat in an easy chair by the window, his head propped up in his hands. He looked the picture of despair, as though the weight of our entire act rested on his shoulders.

We'd come to a seemingly insurmountable problem, one he couldn't fix or change. We wanted to believe that I'd recover, but a little voice kept nagging, *What if the doctor is right? What if nothing ever changes? What then?*

Don't cry. You can't even blow your nose. For once, I welcomed the nurse's return.

While ICU regulations permitted visitors to stay only five minutes per hour, the staff bent the rules and Gary camped out in my room for the next two days. Time revolved around looking at the ceiling and gazing at the floor with my chin in Gary's hands, pain medication and meals. Nothing else mattered.

On the third day, my doctor snapped on the glaring overhead lights and strode over to my bed with two others in tow. When the three of them surrounded me, my heart leaped into my throat as if looking for a safe place to hide. My doctor showed me the fat piece of rubber which was dressed up in the fancy words "endotracheal tube," but that didn't fool me. I recognized a garden hose when I saw one.

"Your chest x-ray looks worse this morning, so I'm going to put you on a respirator," the doctor said.

"You'll start feeling better once you're getting more air. You might not need it for very long. I'll see how your x-ray looks in a couple days. I can do this little procedure right here in your room."

While he spoke, I eyed the garden hose with suspicion, not wanting to believe what he planned to do. I must have passed out when he put the tube down my throat. When I came to, I thought twice before each painful swallow. Looking up at Gary, I opened my mouth, but not even a whispered complaint could emerge. At this point, conversations all but ceased as few people could read my lips.

The garden hose was connected to something called a respirator which occupied a table next to the wall behind me. I couldn't see it, but I could hear its noisy *whoosh-whoosh, whoosh-whoosh* as it pumped air in and out of my lungs. In my new motionless, speechless, horizontal hell, I needed help just to breathe.

Fear became a constant companion. My lungs kept filling with fluid and I had no way to call for help. Whenever this happened, my frantic eyes would search out Gary. Once I made eye contact, his curt statement, "Vickie needs suctioning," brought instant results. My nurse would dash into the room and insert a long, skinny tube down the garden hose into my lungs to vacuum out the secretions.

Later that day my nurse, Laura, came in to do yet another procedure. "Vickie, you won't be able to eat with the endotracheal tube, so I need to put an NG [nasogastric] tube down your nose so we can feed you." As if sensing my unspoken concern, she held it up. "See, it's a lot smaller in diameter than the other one. It won't be nearly as painful going down."

<hr />

At some point, my eyes focused on the sight of my parents and two of my aunts huddled around the bed. Mom's swollen red eyes betrayed her anguish. They had just returned from a vacation, and the shock of my appearance and condition had turned their faces chalky white. They tried making small talk to break the tension, but I could sense their deep concern.

As night approached again, my fear increased. I knew that Gary needed to get some sleep, but if he left me alone, how would I summon help when I needed suctioning?

Sensing my wide-eyed terror, Gary spent another sleepless night with me. The eerie sounds of the respirator and the flickering lights turned into shadowy ghouls that danced across the walls. A nurse entered the room and marched across the ceiling, comfortable as you please. If I hadn't seen it with my own eyes, I wouldn't have believed it. Meanwhile powerful, mind-bending narcotics kept dripping into my veins.

The following morning two nurses wheeled a much welcomed change into the room. When plugged into a wall outlet, the Clinitron® bed contained tiny beads that stayed in constant motion. This change meant no more turns.

◆━◆━◆━◆━◆━◆

By the end of the first week, a monotonous routine had established itself. Mornings started around 4:30 a.m. when I heard the portable x-ray machine lumber down the hall so the technician could snap another shot of my lungs.

A few hours later my respiratory doctor would appear to perform a broncoscopy. Sending his lighted tube down the garden hose allowed him to look directly into my lungs and to pull out secretions too deep for regular suctioning.

Next, a PT would arrive armed with a long list of exercises. She claimed that the initials stood for Physical Therapist, but I knew better as the Pain and Torture dragged on. Movements as simple as shrugging my shoulders ten times left me completely exhausted.

In the afternoon Gary or my mother or one of my aunts would read to me. This, along with mail call, became a high point. Cards and letters had begun to pour in from concerned friends and relatives—a cheerful reminder that someone outside those four walls cared.

On day nine of my hospital stay, I looked forward to my upcoming operation—a tracheostomy. A doctor would remove the garden hose from my mouth, slit my throat and insert a tube directly into my neck.

When I awakened, it felt like a herd of elephants had galloped through my throat. It remained tender for days, but the change did allow me to start eating real food again. Marlene, one of my favorite nurses, brought me some chocolate pudding: my flavor-starved taste buds did back flips all afternoon!

Her warm smile and special care made the next shift that much harder to bear. I took an instant dislike to the "stick to the rules no matter what" night nurse as soon as I saw her.

"Well, OK," Inga said to my mom, "you can stay if you sit over there in the corner and promise not to bother her."

Mom and I looked at each other in stunned disbelief after this crabby nurse flounced out of the room. She obviously did not understand that Mom had volunteered to spend her nights in my hospital room to summon help when I couldn't breathe.

My sleepless nights in ICU rated right up there with root canals. When Mom got ready to go down to the cafeteria for her customary 3 a.m. snack that night, she figured out, with some smooth lip-guessing, that I wanted something to eat too. When the sandwich-toting "renegade" returned with a bacon, lettuce and tomato on toast, we felt like two kids plotting a raid on the cookie jar. While she fed me my half, Mom kept a vigilant lookout for the "enemy."

Despite my tender throat, I savored every bite. Maybe the fear of getting caught made it taste better, but that BLT became the high point of my entire nineteen-day stay. Much to our relief, the grouchy nurse did not catch us nor did she find out about our wee-hours feast since we swallowed all the evidence.

My eyes popped open early. *Moving day!* I'd finally "weaned" off the respirator and today I looked forward to the big move. Gary's report of roomy therapy gyms, large windows in patients' rooms and a heated therapy pool danced through my mind. I pictured myself zipping down the halls of the "rehab center," and wondered how long it would take to get back on my feet so I could get on with my life. *Let's get this show on the road!*

CHAPTER EIGHT

Let the Rehab Begin

◆━◆━◆━◆━◆

"I wish you all the best, Vickie!" I smiled and thanked Marlene.

"Nothing personal, but *don't* come back and see us."

"At least not as a patient," another nurse added.

"You better believe I won't!"

With that, the ambulance attendants rolled me out of ICU. At the hospital's entrance, automatic doors parted, the cart clattered across a patch of cement, and an explosion of sights, sounds and colors bombarded my sluggish senses. A cool breeze caressed my fevered cheeks. The sweet chirp of house finches seemed to reach clear into my soul. Then the cart slid into a waiting ambulance, doors slammed shut and the moment—forever etched in my memory—was gone.

When we reached Craig Hospital, Gary joined us just inside the entrance. One elevator ride later, I rolled into my new room. A shiver of excitement raced through me. Someone drew a curtain around the bed and efficient hands made quick work of the transfer. Once the nurse finished checking me in, all sorts of people flocked into the room—and not one of them wore white! Amidst the doctors, nurses, therapists and aides who introduced themselves, I didn't remember a single name.

Why am I so tired? It's all I can do just to lie here.

When the last person left, a man with coal-black hair appeared. His Chinese accent matched his features. "Hello, Vickie. I'm Kwan. I'm one of the respiratory therapists on your team." He turned. "And you are . . ."

"Gary." My husband stuck out his hand. "I'm Vickie's husband. Glad to meet you."

I yawned and closed my eyes.

"Vickie, wake up! I need to do a test on you."

I opened one eye and mouthed the words, "Go away!"

"Not until you do this for me."

I gasped. *This guy can read lips?*

Kwan laughed and I knew that we would become good friends. While he tested my breathing capacity, I realized with a start that this tiny room had no windows to the outside. Later I learned that the hospital had expanded years ago and exchanged the windows for a gymnasium. This explained why veterans referred to Room 301 as "The Pit." I couldn't agree more.

Shortly after Kwan left, a loud voice boomed in my ear.

"Vickie Baker!"

Reluctantly I opened my eyes. A tall man with thinning brown hair and a stethoscope slung around his neck leaned over my bed.

"I'm Dr. Wicks. I'll be your respiratory doctor." He straightened and turned toward Gary. "Are you Vickie's husband?"

After they shook hands, the doctor continued. "Your vital capacity is only 700 CCs, so I'm going to put you back on the respirator."

My spirits sank. *Nooo!*

"Since you're having a little trouble breathing, this should help you feel better. Do you have any questions?"

I sighed. "No."

"OK, then I'll see you tomorrow," Dr. Wicks said as he turned to leave. "Kwan will be in to get you set up."

Kwan soon appeared with the necessary equipment and hooked up miles of now-familiar blue tubing to the hardware still in my neck. Disappointment mingled with tears when I heard the *whoosh-whoosh* that now chimed in chorus with the symphony of sounds coming from the other two machines in the room.

❖❖❖❖❖

Later, I looked up when a sandy-haired man approached.

"Hello, I'm Chaplain Stewart. Would this be a good time for me to stop in?"

"Sure," Gary mumbled with an unconvincing smile. "But Vickie can't talk with the trach."

Which is fine with me. I have about as much interest in God as—

He has in you, the voice of evil interjected.

I tried to smile, but the corners of my mouth seemed to have frozen in a permanent downward curve.

The chaplain made small talk with Gary, where were we from, what had brought me to Craig, etc. I saw new worry lines on Gary's face. The strain of these past three weeks showed in the dark circles under his eyes. My dull mind wandered until a comment yanked me back to the present.

"I'll come back and check on you again."

The two men shook hands.

The chaplain started toward the door, then stopped. Turned. With great hesitation he spoke. "We have services here every Sunday morning at 10:30 down in the chapel. You're both welcome to attend."

Yeah, right.

Two days later, my nurse, Chris, burst into the room after lunch. "Are you ready to start getting up and getting out of this room?"

You bet I am!

"You're going to get rid of those tongs today—"

About time!

"And get a halo."

Say what?

"Ginny and Corrine should be here any minute," Chris continued. "Once they attach the halo, you can start getting up in a chair."

Bells and whistles went off in my head. *Attach?*

And "attach" they did—with four wicked-looking bolts screwed directly into my skull. I felt very little pain. (I guess there are advantages to being hardheaded.) Next, two black rods, directly within my line of vision, screwed onto the front of a hard plastic vest lined with sheepskin, which I would wear for the next five weeks.

Dinner that night brought an agonizing setback.

Gary had fed me only two spoonfuls of soup when I gasped and attempted to cough. After Jill, one of my respiratory therapists, dashed in to suction me, my evening nurse, Fay, discovered that the halo prevented me from swallowing right. Instead of sending food down to my stomach, I aspirated it into my lungs. Moments later, she returned with a detestable feeding tube.

The following week I started weaning off the respirator and, at last, I could see a flicker of life at the end of the pit.

◆◆◆◆

Blinding sun beats down mercilessly. Hushed voices speak. "She's bleeding. Her temp is 105. Better ice her down." Words fade. Something cool touches my face. Brushes my cheeks, my forehead. Dances fleetingly across my cracked lips. A smile, a friendly word and my confusion temporarily lifts.

I looked up into the face of Paula, my evening aide, as she continued applying cool washcloths to my body. Her soothing actions lulled me to sleep.

Some time later, I opened my eyes. A sunbeam danced across the blanket. *The Pit doesn't have windows. Where am I?*

Gary sat in a chair opposite the window. When he saw me awake, he walked over to my bed and spoke. "You're in the Intensive Care Unit of Swedish Hospital. It connects to Craig by way of a long hallway. You had a massive upper G.I. bleed and a high fever.

"You were making such good progress when this happened." Gary's voice cracked and he turned away.

My face must have mirrored his as we both struggled with the latest blow fate had dealt. At that point, I wanted to check out of the game called life. I found out later that Gary tried to do just that. Thank God he didn't succeed.

———◆———◆———◆———

Twelve days later, I overheard Gary talking to his father on the phone. After he hung up, I looked at him and glanced over at our fancy communication device.

"You have a question?"

I blinked once.

Gary held up the travel-worn piece of cardboard and pointed to the top row of handwritten letters. In the third row down, I blinked. He moved his finger across. I blinked on the middle letter, "M." He repeated the procedure until I had spelled out the words, "Move today?"

"Yes."

Soon, capable hands rolled the bed and the ever-present respirator and IV pole through the narrow underground tunnel. My puny reflection, framed by the hefty metal halo, mocked me from the shiny overhead slats.

When we reached my old room in The Pit, I learned that one of my roommates had gone home and that I had first dibs on his "parking spot." I could now look out the open door to observe the comings and goings at the nurses' station. In a world that lacked movement and speech, this new location counted big time.

Soon, two familiar figures approached. "Well, look who they let in here," Dr. Wicks kidded.

"Hi, Vickie, it's good to have you back!" Jill exclaimed. Jill's friendly, caring nature began in her heart, twinkled in her eyes and culminated in the broad smile that came into view.

"Thanks," I mouthed.

Dr. Wicks listened to my lungs and allowed me to start weaning again—twenty minutes twice a day.

A couple mornings later I awakened to the words, "Are you crazy?"

Blinking, I tried to clear the cobwebs from my sleepy brain. The voice sounded familiar enough.

The doctor I'd nicknamed "Dr. Presto"—now you see him, now you don't—barged into my dreams every morning during his rounds. But his unusually kind greeting stumped me. *Huh?*

"Are you crazy, refusing my orders?" his gruff voice continued.

Then it hit me—the drug. The new drug that I'd refused to take last night. Fortunately, Gary arrived so he did my talking for me. This impatient, important doctor didn't have time to play "guess the word" games with silent patients like me.

"You never came back to explain what this new medication is and why Vickie needs to take it," Gary reminded him.

"Oh, yeah," Dr. Presto muttered with a wave of his hand, as if trying to shoo away a pesky fly. "I'm starting you on Daricon twice a day. It prevents smooth muscle spasms caused by an indwelling catheter."

Before Gary could ask about potential side effects, Dr. Presto had disappeared out the door in his typical "I don't have time for this nonsense" style.

Over the next few weeks I got rid of the halo, which allowed me to start eating again, but the sight of food made me nauseous. Because of the blood transfusions I'd received in ICU, I now had Hepatitis C.

It's not fair! my mind screamed. *It's just not fair!*

Judy, my physical therapist, had been coming into my room to work with me. But three-and-a-half weeks after my arrival, I would finally sit up in a wheelchair and go to the gym for PT. Talk about team effort!

After my aide dressed me, Jill appeared pushing a cart with a portable respirator and Judy arrived with one of the hospital's "clunkers." I didn't care that it was big and bulky, that sweet chariot had come to sweep me off my feet! Soon, two orderlies arrived, along with my parents.

After the orderlies transferred me, Judy pushed the chair, Gary wheeled the IV pole and Jill brought up the rear with her cart. Before we reached the door, a roar like ocean waves pounding the shore filled my ears right before I passed out—my introduction to the hypotension (abnormally low blood pressure) "dizzies." When I regained consciousness, Judy slowly lowered the front tires back down to the floor—the first of many tip-backs.

When we pulled into the third-floor gymnasium, I saw a jumble of bright colors with wheelchairs zipping past, people exercising on padded tables, sunshine, laughter and lively music. The other patients' upbeat attitudes puzzled me. I saw nothing to smile about.

The next morning, my aide arrived at 6:00 to feed me and dress me before 9:00 "mat class" in the gym. After a few bites of breakfast, my stomach revolted with dry heaves—a common occurance since I'd started eating solid food again. Gary, who spent entire days by my side and had no money coming in, finished off my sweet roll.

"Hello," I half-whispered, half-spoke.

I can talk!

"The hole in your throat will close up in a day or two," Kwan said. "Then you can go in the pool."

"Now that you're off the respirator," my nurse added, "I'll see if we can move you out of here. How would you like a room with a window?"

I stared at her in awe. "You can do that?"

Deep in slumber the following morning, a thought gnawed at the edge of consciousness. *She never recovered.* I awakened with a start.

Who never recovered?

My eyes popped open as memory of the move overshadowed the fuzzy question mark planted by sleep. A soft glow from the predawn sky spilled through a large pane of glass in the corner of my new private room. Pale pink fingers of light gradually turned magenta as the fiery ball of sun made its grand entrance.

Meanwhile, the lump in the pit of my stomach grew. *Who didn't recover? Someone I met?* Then it hit me. Of course! The woman in the video. Yesterday during "chair class," instead of having us do exercises, the therapist let us stay in the gym and watch "horror" movies. I had naively believed that none could top last week's "skin flick" which featured patients with huge gaping holes in their ankles, bottoms or sides where the flesh had been eaten away clear down to the bone. The message? Pressure sores can kill, so when you're sitting up, remember to do your weight shifts!

Yet that movie was nothing compared to the one which shattered my carefully laid plans for the future. I could no longer tap dance around the truth. I would no longer dance at all.

The former patient who starred in this video demonstrated how she managed various tasks—fixing meals, doing laundry, etc. But I only saw the wheelchair and the curled-up fingers. Her spinal cord injury, the same level as mine, had occurred over fifteen years ago, yet *she never recovered.*

Wake up, Vickie! What makes you think your fate will be any different?

Certainly no one else gave us reason to hope. Doctors pegged me a "C 5-6 quad." The staff accepted this permanent diagnosis as a fact of life with a casual, "what's the big deal?" attitude. Over the past two months, my dream of walking and my hope of sailing through the air with the greatest of ease faded. The previous day's eye-opening film had killed those dreams.

Maybe I'd been conning myself all along. Perhaps Gary had too. Like two ostriches neck-deep in sand, Gary and I gradually stopped talking about my recovery, trapeze and the future in general. I kept my fears to myself on the off chance that I could learn to walk—if I wanted to badly enough. That my fingers would start working—if only I concentrated harder. That the paralysis might completely go away—if I just had enough hope.

She never recovered. A chill crept down my spine.

PART THREE

Swing Forward

CHAPTER NINE

The Real World

oday's the day! On that bright September morning, my physical therapist doodled, my nurse fidgeted and my occupational therapist finished filling out paperwork. Gary kept glancing at the clock. Me, I just stared straight ahead, trying to collect my scattered thoughts.

Will Gary still love me? I feel so useless . . . I can't even dress myself anymore.

A relentless army of "what ifs" and "I can'ts" marched through my head, but Gary's smile reassured me. Excitement mingled with fear. Finally the door burst open and my doctor swept into the room.

Let the discharge conference begin!

"Vickie's level of injury is C 5-6," my PT began. "She has radial wrist extensors but not flexors."

So I can raise my hands when my palms face down. Big deal!

Judy continued. "She has no skin breakdown at this time. Her motor and sensory tests show . . ."

Half-listening, I looked out the window and watched a squirrel scamper up a tree. I didn't need professionals to remind me of the sorry shape of my body or what I could and could not do anymore. I knew better than they did! I had no sensation from my upper chest down to my gimpy toes. I could not walk, use my fingers, dress myself, transfer in or out of my chair, cook a simple meal, swing on a trapeze or do about anything else I could think of. *Will anything ever change? The doctors certainly don't seem to think so.*

After the others took their turn and my doctor began to speak, I tuned back in.

"In summary, Vickie has had multiple medical complications."

You can say that again.

"Her weight is eighty-four and she's eating fairly well. Her husband has been thoroughly instructed in her care—changing her catheter, doing her daily bowel program. He will turn her every three hours at night. They will live in their converted Greyhound bus. Any questions? No? Then this conference is over."

I'm out of here!

Packing all the knicknacks I'd acquired over the past three months seemed to take forever, but at last I sat outside. Gary pulled the car around, scooped me out of my chair and set me down in the bucket seat. I felt safe and secure in his strong arms.

He tied a long webbed belt around the back of the seat to keep me from tumbling forward if we stopped suddenly, buckling it snuggly around my upper chest. "Dizzy?" he asked.

"No. For once I feel OK."

After collapsing my wheelchair, Gary stowed it in back. The slam of the hatchback door had a pleasant ring to it. The big moment had finally arrived. "Ready?"

I smiled back. "More than ready."

"We need to stop at the store, first. I ran out of milk yesterday—and what do you want for dinner?"

I gave a nervous laugh.

"What?"

"I was just thinking—we make a great team. You don't like to cook and I don't like to eat. Dinner . . . what do you dislike fixing the least?"

Gary grinned. "How about grilled hamburgers?"

"Fine with me."

When Gary dashed into the store, I noticed a stooped-over man shuffling toward his car with a loaded shopping cart. His snow-white hair made him appear ancient. *In his eighties? Nineties? Man, that guy can drive himself to the store and buy his own groceries. How come he can do that and I can't? It's not fair!*

Moments later Gary reappeared and soon we pulled up to the bus.

"Man, it's good to be home." The bright blue-and-white striped awning beckoned to me.

Gary started dinner and the smell of burgers on the grill piqued my appetite. *Home cooking!* I watched Gary pop open another beer. *Uh-oh. How many does that make?*

After dinner, Gary left my chair outside under the awning, picked me up and carried me to bed. The loneliness, pain and fear I'd carried around with me all summer slowly melted away. Our long months of separation seemed a distant memory as I lay in Gary's arms. I stared into the darkness long after I heard Gary's deep rhythmic breathing and pondered the uncertainty of the future.

The next morning Gary dressed me and carried me up front to the living room. Unable to budge an inch if my life depended on it, I sat on the couch where he had placed me and looked at all our handiwork. The custom-made kitchen counter I'd helped Gary construct now housed boxes of medical supplies. Bags of who knows what spilled over into the living room. There was clutter as far as the eye could see and I couldn't do a thing about it.

I hate being so dependent! my mind screamed dozens of times that day. Then I spied a crumpled pair of hand guards—mine—peeking out from behind our swivel chair. My breath caught in my throat and I looked away.

That afternoon while I sat outside in the shade, my parents' car pulled up. When they parked and opened the door, a white streak of fluff leapt out and raced over to me. I'm not sure who enjoyed the reunion more—Fliffus, Gary or me. Overjoyed, our poodle bounded back and forth between us, showering us with big, wet doggy kisses.

"Fliffus, come."

She dashed over and let me pet her. I glanced away, saw a blur of white run past and realized that my hand now stroked nothing but air.

The next day Gary and I became well acquainted with aisle seven—frozen dinners—at the local supermarket.

"Good thing we have a microwave," he said as he loaded up the cart. *Yeah, or we wouldn't eat anything at all.*

One morning, Gary dug out a nifty little device the rehab hospital had sent home with me. *Welcome to Buttoning 101.* I slid the stiff, plastic-coated metal band over my hand and attempted to push the protruding wire hook through a button hole in my shirt. The goal? To pull a corresponding button back through the opening. Simple, right?

"Ouch!" I yelped moments later, tears springing to my eyes.

Gary looked up. "What happened?"

"I hooked the inside of my nose."

I'll never get it right! Why does everything have to be so hard?

On Saturday, as we made the trip to Bruce's, a part of me looked forward to it, but another part of me cringed. In the car, my overactive imagination recreated the miracle which happened so effortlessly in my dreams and was so sweet in my fantasies.

Ecstatic over my recovery, I stand high above the ground on the pedestal. Leaping up, my body slices through the air. I give it my all, working hard to punch a hole in the sky with my toes. I can almost feel the catcher's firm grip on my legs as we connect on a two-and-a-half. With my heart pounding and my adrenaline pumping, we swing away.

The car stopped and Gary cut the ignition, breaking my reverie. While he set up the clunky wheelchair, I stared at my useless hands with their lifeless, curled-up fingers that would never again hold a flybar tight in their grasp—or anything else for that matter. A lone tear squeezed out. With the back of one hand I quickly brushed it away.

"Hi, Vickie! Hi, Gary!" Bruce called from the pedestal. "I'm glad you could make it."

Looking up, I gave Bruce a clumsy wave. Sunlight glinted off one of the magnificent uprights. I watched Tony grab the flybar and take off, as smooth and graceful as a bird.

Welcome to the real world, Little Circus Girl.

My mouth felt as dry as the sawdust that I would never again feel under my feet. Gary pushed me into the backyard. My wheelchair seemed as out of place as a clown at a funeral. The other fliers on the ground made small talk with me, but outside of the hospital setting they seemed to feel as uncomfortable as I did. If I couldn't handle my disability, how could I expect them to?

With my emotions stretched as tight as our trapeze net, the tear-jerking, dizzy-grey days of fall passed. With the last of our dwindling savings Gary and I made plans to drive the bus down to Florida for the winter so I could spend time wheeling outside to build up my strength.

We planned to have Thanksgiving dinner with my parents and leave the next day, but an approaching blizzard changed our schedule. When I called Mom to tell her that we needed to leave today, she and my dad drove over to say good-bye. To complicate matters, Fliffus ran away. Gary spent all morning searching, but we finally ran out of time. Mom's promise to look for her after we left did little to ease the pain that had settled in my heart. Dad seemed close to tears when we hugged good-bye and a sense of impending doom washed over me.

Is this move really a good idea? I feel so helpless. I'll be dependent on Gary for everything. Can he handle this?

Gary cranked up the bus and made one final check outside. I looked up when he came back, but he shook his head—no Fliffus. The wind shrieked, chilling me to the bone.

Mentally, I reviewed the checklist while Gary took care of the tasks we had once shared. *Awning rolled up and secured. Bus unplugged. Water hoses and cables coiled up, stowed in the possum-bellies below. Phone company notified. Phone unplugged.*

Grey water drained. Compartments locked. Car hitched up.

Sitting motionless on the couch, I listened for Fliffus and missed her terribly when we pulled out. The following week I learned that she'd been hit by a truck.

Palm trees waved their bushy fronds, extending a warm Florida greeting. I drank in the balmy breezes, basked in the sun's healing warmth and marveled at the picture-postcard view that had drawn us here.

"This was a good move," I said over dinner that first night. "I'll be able to wheel outside every day and I'll learn to do more for myself." *Then you'll stop drinking.* "I'm glad we came."

Gary looked out over the lake. "Me too."

Just then, a woman walked by pushing a stroller. She stopped to talk to a couple sunning themselves on their patio. I watched her toddler climb out of his stroller, unzip his windbreaker and take it off. *Even a two-year-old can do more than me. It's not fair!*

After lunch, the real work began when Gary tugged gloves onto my uncooperative hands and I headed over the paved lane to the office to check the mail. Gary walked with me the first few times.

"I can't believe how flat these roads are, yet how hard it is to push," I gasped fifteen minutes later when I stopped to rest. The few blocks that separated our lot from the office, a mere hop, skip and a stroll away, took on monumental proportions. "Why does everything have to be so hard?"

"Want me to push the rest of the way?" Gary asked.

Yes, yes, yes! my exhausted body screamed in my ears.

"No," I rasped through gritted teeth. "We're almost there."

In no time, our friendly neighbors got used to watching me huff and puff past their trailers. A few months down the road, Betty, a neighbor three lots down, hailed me over when I huffed past.

"Vickie, we go to a prayer meeting every Wednesday night at the clubhouse. We'd like for you to come with us tonight. Will you?"

A prayer meeting? What's that?

"It's very informal," she continued. "About seven or eight of our Christian brothers and sisters come to the meetings."

People get together to pray?

"It starts at 7:00. We can push you over there."

Not able to think up a plausible excuse, I accepted.

Gary and I had just finished eating when Betty and her husband, Tom, approached.

"We're kidnapping your wife," Tom joked.

"Have fun."

You bet.

When we got there, Betty introduced me to the three other couples who had already arrived.

I smiled, nodded and wondered when I would learn to just say no.

Tom opened the meeting and everyone whipped out a notebook and pen. *What? They take notes?*

Each person spoke about friends, relatives and situations that needed prayer. They also shared good news—for which they gave God all the credit.

My mind wandered out the door and back to the bus. Gary had become distant lately. He didn't seem to sleep much anymore. He never smiled. I felt like such a burden to him. No one would ever guess that less than a year ago he had dropped his drawers—on a regular basis—in a comedy trapeze act.

Suddenly, the sound of my name being called yanked me back to the present. I jerked my head up. Eight pairs of pity-filled eyes bored into me. "I'm sorry," I mumbled. "What did you say?"

"Vickie, we believe that it is God's will that you be healed."

You barely know me!

"We would like to pray for your healing." Nods and "amens" filled the room. Then everyone stood up.

What now? Are they going to gang up on me? I watched as they closed in. *Bingo.* Shrinking down in my chair, I wished myself invisible. Hands reached out; pity flowed freely.

"Dear heavenly Father," Tom began, "we thank You for the opportunity to come before You today on behalf of Your precious child, Vickie. . . ."

In spite of myself, a slender thread of hope squeezed into my hardened heart. *Is it possible that God cares about me? That He might even consider healing me? These folks seem to think so. They can't all be wrong, can they?*

Then the voice of evil overpowered those thoughts. *Who are you trying to kid, Little Circus Girl? God could care less whether you're alive or dead.*

Their words fell on unhearing ears, met with eyes blinded to the truth. When Tom finished speaking and the last "Amen!" faded away, eyes stared down at me expectantly. Nothing happened. Apparently no one had penciled me into God's schedule for a 7 p.m. healing that muggy spring night. One by one the do-gooders drifted away. Tom and Betty pushed me back to the bus and Gary carried me inside.

After he put me to bed that night, I drowned my dashed hopes in lonely tears. Gary stayed up front with Beethoven's Ninth and beer—lots of it. We didn't seem to have any words left for each other. If only we could talk, confide, share the grief locked up in our hearts. But I found that too risky. *Don't rock the boat. Don't cause waves. You need him a lot more than he needs you.*

Later that night, I heard the front door open and close. The sound of our car driving off slammed into my consciousness like a fist. *Another late-night beer run.* My heart pounded in my ears as worry battled fear for control. *What if he gets in an accident and doesn't come back?* A river of tears later, the car returned. The front door opened. I would live to cry another night.

Ten days later, Gary purchased two airline tickets for Denver. Mine was one-way.

CHAPTER TEN

Hanging On
by a Thread

—◆—◆—◆—◆—

Sandy pulled up to the entrance and parked. When she hoisted my chair out of the back of her car and set it up, I chuckled, thinking back to our first shopping expedition. After Gary had brought me back from Florida, I'd stayed with my parents for two months. Sandy had become my morning attendant.

That day, Mom and Dad had watched from the sidelines, joined by a neighbor who exclaimed, "She can't do that! She doesn't have any muscles!" None of them had believed that this petite woman, who weighed ninety-two pounds and stood all of five foot two, could possibly transfer me all by herself into her car. Had she ever proved them wrong!

After another efficient transfer, Sandy pushed me into the admissions office. A woman behind the desk looked up when we approached.

"I'm here for reevaluation," I said.

"Want me to get you up the same time tomorrow?" Sandy asked.

"Yes. I need to be here by 9:00 all week."

I watched her drive away, feeling terribly alone—even if I did know half the staff here at Craig. Once I had the paperwork, I wheeled across the hall to the clinic, hooked an arm around my push handle and leaned sideways to clear my lightheadedness.

After a brief wait I heard my name called and followed the nurse into an examining room. In short order, I lay on a padded table shivering under nothing but a sheet. A few minutes later, the door flew open.

"Hello, I'm Dr. Lammertse," said a friendly voice.

I looked up to see a well-groomed man with a closely trimmed beard, small round specs, warm eyes and a smile to match. His flashy bow-tie added the perfect touch. "I'll be your doctor. Would you like a blanket?" he asked when he saw me inching the sheet up over my nose with my teeth.

"Yes! Thank you."

"I see this is your first reevaluation," he said, studying my inch-thick file. "How has your health been?" Dr. Lammertse patiently listened while I told him about my pneumonia-free winter in Florida.

After the exam, the nurse dressed me and an orderly helped her whisk me back into my chair. Only forty-five minutes remained for me to get upstairs and eat lunch before my afternoon appointment. I pulled up to the elevator to push the button, but suddenly two hands covered my eyes. "Guess who."

"Kwan!" I couldn't mistake his accent anywhere.

The hands retreated. "How are you doing, Vickie? Have you been staying healthy?"

"Yeah."

"I'm glad to hear that. How's Gary doing?"

"OK. . . ." I briefly mentioned Florida and that Gary had driven the bus back last month and I'd moved back in with him. "In fact," I added with a grin, "we're making plans to go back out with a circus."

"No kidding!"

"Yeah. Some friends of ours would like to perform in a flying act with Gary. They would travel with us and help take care of me. We're excited." I glanced down at my watch. "Man, if this elevator doesn't get here soon, I'm taking the stairs!"

"*I'll* take you up the stairs," Kwan volunteered.

"I bet you a dollar you won't."

"You're on!" Kwan grabbed my chair and away we went. At the base of the steps, he turned me around, tipped the lightweight chair backward and began to pull me up. The *thump, thump, thump* of our passage echoed in the deserted stairwell. When we emerged from the doorway on the third floor, I half expected a band of roving stair-police to charge over, slap our wrists and issue a citation for unlawful climbing. But to my relief, no one even noticed us.

After I finished that afternoon, a blast of warm air and a fragrant aroma greeted me when the automatic doors sprang open. *I did it! My first solo trip—and I survived!* I wheeled out into the hot July sunshine and spotted our little yellow Honda turning into the ambulance entrance.

Gary drove up and cut the engine. A broad smile lit up his face.

"Gee, trapeze practice must have gone pretty well today," I observed.

"Yeah. I'll tell you about it on the way home. How was your first day?"

"Great! I made a new friend. Dale is a quad with the same level of injury as mine and she has a service dog that's trained to help her. You'll probably get a chance to meet her and Percy later this week."

Halfway home, I remembered. "Say, when we get back to the bus, I need you to put a dollar in my backpack for me. I, um, lost a bet today. And Kwan said to tell you 'hi.' "

❖❖❖❖❖

"This is John," my nurse said the following morning. "He'll be taking you over on a cart for your IVP."

Lying on my back, I stared at my reflection in the shiny slats above my head as the cart rumbled through the tunnel that connected Craig to Swedish Hospital. I recalled my last underground trip and shuddered, thinking about all of the hardware that had been attached to me. *A halo, a feeding tube, an IV and worst of all, the trach. One year ago I couldn't even breathe on my own! I'm glad* that's *behind me.*

When we reached the radiology department, someone ushered us into a small room and helped John transfer me onto a padded table. "I'll be back when you're done."

A few minutes later I heard footsteps. A burly man with bushy black eyebrows and friendly eyes introduced himself. "Let's see . . . you've had an intervenous pylogram before, haven't you?" He flipped through some papers.

I gulped. "A what?"

"An IVP."

"Oh, yeah. I had one last summer."

"Did you have any adverse side effects? Feel flushed? Start getting a headache? Get nauseous?"

"No, nothing."

"Good." He lowered the x-ray machine from the ceiling, flipped on a light and moved the table on which I lay, while explaining the procedure to me. "Now that I've lined up your kidneys under this light, I need to inject some dye."

He pulled up my shirt sleeve and opened an alcohol swab. I turned away. When he finished, I relaxed and let my mind wander.

Suddenly I gasped. Opening my mouth, I tried to pull air into my lungs. "Doctor, I'm . . . I'm having trouble breathing!" *Something's wrong! I need more air! What's happening?* The room spins. Anxious faces peer down. Panic bubbles to the surface. Voices . . . loud voices . . . footsteps . . . running. *Hurry!* Hands . . . lots of hands. *Do something!*

Shouting . . . voices shouting, "I don't get a BP, doctor." Deep voice booms, "Get a crash cart—STAT!" From far away, "We're losing her. . . ." Darkness descends.

◆◆◆◆◆

Eyes flicker open . . . try to focus . . . strange ceiling . . . sunset . . . incredible pain . . . throat throbs . . . excruciating to swallow . . . confusion . . . *Where? What?* Turn away from window. Look into Gary's eyes but can't speak . . . Tube in throat . . . Gary talking . . . eyes close . . . sleep overpowers.

A bright lemon sun lit the room. I felt unrelenting pain. My throat screamed in silent agony. I opened my eyes and looked around. *A hospital room? Why am I here?* Gary walked into the room. A vague memory of an earlier conversation planted question marks. My eyes pleaded for answers. He patiently explained—again.

"You had a severe reaction to the IVP dye yesterday. You stopped breathing and your heart stopped beating. You—you almost didn't make it."

My eyes widened.

He continued. "That's why you're here. That's why the tube is in your throat, but it will come out later today."

Thank goodness.

"When your doctor called, he told me you'd been in the ER for over an hour—and that you were still in a coma."

A coma?

Gary's voice dropped and he turned away. "He wasn't very optimistic that you'd pull through."

After Gary left, his words haunted me. *Is there a reason I'm still alive? Is God—*

God has nothing to do with this, Little Circus Girl, a voice hissed from the corner of my mind. *Doctors resuscitated you—that's all.*

I fell into a troubled sleep.

Morning again. Overcast, gloomy. Gary arrived—saw the respirator back in the room, the tube back in my mouth. A nurse walked in and told me—told both of us. "You have staph infection in your lungs. You might be here for a few more days."

A few more days! Tears squeezed out of my eyes. Soundless screams burst through unmoving lips.

Six days later the detestable tube came out of my throat when a surgeon performed a tracheostomy. Once again, doctors, nurses, therapists and aides became key players in my life.

"Vickie Baker," a familiar voice boomed.

I looked up.

"We've got to stop meeting like this," Dr. Wicks, my pulmonologist, joked. He listened to my lungs and talked about recent chest x-rays. "I'm increasing your weaning time to four hours, twice a day. How does that sound?"

I smiled my approval. Two weeks after I'd rolled into intensive care, my doctor booked me a room at Craig. With the help of aides, orderlies and Gary, my hospital bed rumbled through the tunnel. Déjà vu struck when I glared at my gimpy reflection—complete with respirator and miles of blue tubing. I sighed. *Back to square one.*

Shortly after I rolled into Room 301, Kwan, my respiratory therapist for the day, came in to give me a breathing treatment.

"Hi, Kwan. Vickie has something for you." Gary reached into my backpack.

Kwan stared at the crumpled envelope with his name scrawled across the front. "What's this?"

"Open it."

He held up the dollar bill, puzzled.

"You don't remember the bet Vickie made with you? That day she didn't want to wait for the elevator?"

Kwan's face lit up. He ran out of the room waving the money over his head shouting, "I won! I won!" But moments later he returned. "Dr. Wicks took it away from me and gave it to Tanya—out at the nurses' station—and she won't give it back."

With his head hanging down, he looked like a forlorn puppy who had just lost his master. I laughed. Trust Kwan to lighten the mood.

That night I felt hot, miserable and confused. An infection put me back on the respirator—full time. At midnight I lay awake with my tiny TV turned on for company, feeling like something even a cat wouldn't drag home. Suddenly, my doctor waltzed through the door.

Man, this fever must be worse than I thought. Doctors don't visit patients in the middle of the night. I must be hallucinating.

I closed my eyes and slowly reopened them, but Dr. Lammertse—in the flesh—still stood there reading my chart. His words did not stick, but his concern that night remains indelibly etched in my memory.

In the days to come, time slowed to a crawl. My parents visited every day, anxious to do whatever they could to help. One day I took Mom up on her offer.

Through trial and error, Mom deciphered my silent lip movements. "You want me to make ten shoe? No . . . ten . . . not ten . . . tea? Tea . . . shirt? You want me to make a T-shirt?"

I smiled. *Yes!*

She finally translated the rest of my urgent request with a look of dismay. "You want me to make a T-shirt for Ted? Your teddy bear?"

I nodded.

"And you want me to embroider the words, 'Craig Survivor 1985' across the front?"

I nodded again, knowing full well what would follow.

"But I can't sew!"

I just smiled. I knew better. So far, she had designed—and sewn—four pairs of pants for me, three fabric legbag covers that I wore when I had shorts on, plus a couple of other miscellaneous inventions I'd thought up since then. A few days later Ted proudly sat on my bed showing off his new threads.

Finally, a full week after the infection put me on the respirator full time, Dr. Wicks proclaimed that I could wean off the respirator for half an hour, twice that day.

As days blended into weeks, Gary and I finally faced the facts. One evening, during my precious time off the respirator, Gary pushed me—in one of Craig's comfortable reclining "clunkers"—out to the back patio.

A cool breeze ruffled the leaves on nearby trees and caressed my flushed cheeks. I drew in a deep breath and turned toward Gary. "This is pure heaven. It gets so hot in my room—even with a fan going all the time—and the doctor thinks I might be here a couple more weeks."

"It's hot in the bus," Gary said.

"What?"

"I can't use the air conditioner because it keeps blowing the power in Bruce's house. I don't think we can live in the bus anymore. We need to find a place that's less restrictive for you—so you can wheel around inside. You've already lost most of the strength you gained last winter in Florida."

I surveyed my toothpick arms. "I know . . . say, this might be a good time for you to start looking for a place. Maybe we can find something before I get out."

"That's what I was thinking," Gary said.

We sat in silence for a few minutes. With slumped shoulders, Gary put into words something I already suspected. "I don't think it will work for us to go back on the road. Your health is too fragile."

Late that night, in the darkness and privacy of my hospital room, I cried.

Over the next couple of weeks Gary checked out affordable housing and shared his findings with me every evening. One night he snuck me out of the hospital to look at a nearby townhouse. Soon, he pulled up in front of a cheerful yellow structure.

"It looks so bright and airy!"

"The gate is locked right now," Gary said, "but on the other side of that privacy fence there's a huge backyard that all twelve units share."

While we sat parked on that quiet street, I looked around the quaint neighborhood and gazed at the townhouse. "I want to go inside."

The following week my doctor issued a genuine pass. Gary and I met with the realtor and got a tour of the inside.

Two nights later, forty-four days after my unwanted, unwelcomed debut in the emergency room, Gary and I sat in the deserted therapy gym with my parents and my Uncle Vic. With their financial assistance we finalized the deal.

"Here's to a long and happy future," Uncle Vic said, raising his paper cup of apple juice.

"And good health," Mom added.

Amidst smiles and toasts, I felt a tiny glimmer of hope.

CHAPTER ELEVEN

Hope Flickers

✦◆✦◆✦◆✦

"That's the stupidest thing I ever heard!" I sputtered. "Are you serious? I'll lose *my* benefits if *you* get a job?"

"That's right." Gary let out a sigh. "You'll also get cut off if we keep the bus—unless I'm living in it."

"I don't understand."

Gary lit a cigarette. "None of their rules make much sense. We're only allowed to have one residence, but if we're not living together, the government considers us divorced and I can do whatever I want."

My thoughts spun out of control. I looked out over the backyard from the shade of our newly installed patio awning. "I thought this house would solve so many problems, but it's just creating more. . . . Say, can I get by without the government's help? I know we'd have to pay for attendant care and for my meds every month, but that's it . . . isn't it?"

"No. You're still uninsurable. You might have to give up seeing doctors . . ."

A shiver crept down my spine. "So much for that idea."

"I'm going to have to sell the bus," Gary said. "The quickest way will be for me to go through the man I bought it from in Texas. I'll drive it down to Arlington and stay until Stewart can find a buyer. Until it sells, you'll have to live here by yourself."

"Do you really think I can do that?"

"Sure—once we get the house fixed up. With the waterbed, you don't need to be turned at night anymore. And now that we have a van with a lift, it will be easier for you to go places with other people, even if you can't drive."

Gary continued. "You're entitled to have attendant care twice a day—so we'll need to find an aide who can put you to bed at night . . . and I need to come up with a way for you to operate the phone when you're in bed. But we'll figure it out—you'll see. Have a little faith in yourself."

Yeah, Vickie, have a little faith in yourself.

"When do you want to leave?"

"As soon as the house is ready. Ideally, by the end of October, before I have to worry about the pipes freezing."

Two weeks later, with both fear and determination, I watched Gary drive away.

"Can you think of anything we missed?" Sandy asked that morning.

"Let's see . . . I have lunch and dinner in a basket in the frige that I can reach and lift out with my wrist. I have a jug of water with a straw in it . . . and there's a basin in the roll-in shower for me to empty my legbag. I guess I'm set. . . ."

Sandy picked up my notebook. "I'll write down my home number. Call me if you run into a problem."

I watched her car pull out. *I can do this. I just need to have faith in myself.* When I pulled up to my worktable, my new ten-week-old kitten joined me. Unhappy about having to give up the craft projects I'd done in the past, I had taken up drawing the previous winter. Armed with my handbrace, I opened a drawing tablet and reached for a felt-tip pen. Punkin curled up on top of my half-finished picture.

"Hey, you can't lay there! Go on, beat it! You're not the boss, I am!"

Twelve ounces of fluff gave me a "Wanna bet?" look, yawned, stretched and finally sauntered away. The straw peeking out of my cup caught his attention. He batted it. I reached out a clumsy hand. "No, Punkin! Stop—" We both watched the pretty straw hit the floor.

When darkness descended, I wheeled to the kitchen, popped my dinner into the microwave and spent the next half hour picking at it. *Will food ever taste good again? Mom's chicken and dumplings used to be my favorite! Now it turns into sawdust—like everything else.*

After dinner, I spent the evening reading, watching the clock and worrying. *Uh oh. It's after 9:00. Where is she? Maybe I better call. What if—*

Just then, I heard someone at the door. My neighbor punched in the combination and entered.

"Hi, Vickie. Same routine as last night?"

"Ah, yes, same thing." I licked my dry lips.

"I might need you to talk me through some of the routine," Debbie continued. "I don't know if I'll remember everything Gary showed me last night."

"Sure, Debbie." *Let's hope* I *remember.* An hour later I lay comfortably under covers with a contented guard kitty purring in my ear.

"Is the phone in the right spot?"

I wiggled my wrist under the cord pinned to my nightshirt to pull my mouthstick closer. Then, grabbing it with my teeth, I turned my head and found that I could easily reach the speaker phone, as well as the TV remote Gary had mounted next to it and the environmental control box. I punched "sixteen" and "on." My lamp clicked on and gave a welcome glow.

"Is that it?"

I looked around. "I think so . . ."

Debbie picked up her house keys and flipped off the overhead light. "Give me a call if we forgot anything. I'll be up for another hour."

"Thanks," I said. "And thanks for signing up with my agency so you could work for me."

"No problem."

When the news ended, I turned off the television with a flip of my mouthstick. "G'night, Punkin," I whispered, rubbing the kitten's furry black nose with my chin. I glanced around the neat, orderly room before tapping the "off" button.

"Uh oh."

The room plunged into total darkness.

"I forgot the night-light!"

Inky black nothingness, combined with my overactive imagination, proved a dreadful combination. I played the "what if" game, concocting gruesome problems that promised to kill me off in no time at all—until my left-brain logic kicked in. *Look, it's not the end of the world. You only need to see the phone if you have a problem—which you don't—so shut up and go to sleep!*

What's wrong? My body's distress signal, known as disreflexia, woke me with a start. My head began to pound—just like that time my catheter plugged up in the hospital. *Is that what's wrong?* I squinted hard, trying to decipher the small numbers on my clock. *11 o'clock? Good. Debbie's still awake.*

I grabbed my mouthstick. Surely I could tap two little buttons in the dark to turn on the lamp. Surely I would hit the right combination sooner or later.

Wrong. *OK, new game plan. Dial the telephone in the dark. I tapped what sounded like the right number. It rang.*

"H'lo?" a gruff male voice mumbled.

"Hi, Matt?" I was answered by an affirmative grunt.

"This is Vickie. I'm sorry to call so late, but would you ask Debbie to come back over? I'm, ah . . . having a problem."

A long pause ensued. Finally, the bewildered voice said, "Debbie who?"

"Isn't this Matt?" I squeaked.

"No, this is Mack."

"I'm sorry." I pushed the off button, tapped zero and explained my predicament. The operator patched me through.

This time, the groggy male voice that answered had the correct name and also had a wife named Debbie—good signs indeed. And yes, she agreed to come back over.

A few minutes later I heard footsteps crunching through the gravel outside my window. The front door creaked open and Debbie walked into my bedroom. She flipped on the overhead. I blinked, squinted, pushed number sixteen with my mouthstick and triumphantly hit "on."

We both jumped.

The shrill scream of a siren sounded like it came from inside the house. It did. A motion-detector Gary had purchased for my protection rested on top of a cupboard high in the kitchen. He had plugged it into a module so that I could operate it from bed. Apparently I had tapped number twelve sometime in the dark and hitting the "on" button triggered the switch. I fumbled with my mouthstick, clumsy in my effort to turn it off.

"At least nothing else can go wrong," I said to my sleepy neighbor.

The doorbell gave us both a start. *Now what?* Debbie cautiously crept to the front door. Moments later she reappeared with her husband. He too had heard the alarm and had thought the worst.

Matt left. Debbie stayed. As soon as she pulled back the covers, I spotted the problem.

"I can't believe I forgot to check that."

Debbie lifted my leg off the catheter tube. We heard it start to drain into my night container on the floor.

"Music to my ears," I said with relief.

The next morning after Sandy got me up, I wrote out a detailed checklist for my night aide, while remembering a lesson I'd taken to heart when Gary and I trooped with the circus: Always be prepared!

I stayed busy that winter, proving to the world that I could live by myself. Never mind that I ate little of my sawdust meals or that when I got cold I had to sit in the bathroom under the heat lamp because I couldn't reach the thermostat.

Near the end of January, Gary returned to Denver—minus one bus. I had planned his homecoming for weeks. We would have a nice, prepared ahead of time meal that he would merely need to pop in the oven. Our life together in this new townhouse would start out on the right wheel.

Unfortunately, my well-laid plans went awry a few days before he returned. Respiratory problems sapped my energy, made my low blood pressure plummet and took away any hope I had of flaunting my short-lived independence. When Gary walked through the front door, he gave me a hug. I coughed in his ear and asked for a tip-back.

"How long has this been going on?" he asked.

"Just a couple of days."

"Have you called your respiratory doctor?"

"Well, no. I thought it might clear up on its own—"

"How often has that happened?"

"Well, it hasn't yet, but there's always a first . . ."

Gary frowned. "Still the unrealistic optimist, I see."

After my chest x-ray the following afternoon, Gary sat with me in the examining room. Soon, one of Dr. Wicks' associates sailed through the door. Even though the word "pneumonia" cropped up, the lecture and outcome shocked me.

Gary stopped by the clinic the next morning to pick up my forgotten jacket before visiting Little Miss "Ignore the Problem and It Will Go Away" in Room 301.

For the next ten days the staff entertained me with round-the-clock breathing treatments. Meanwhile, Gary shopped for a home computer with a good graphics program, convinced that it would help me with my artistic endeavors.

When my lungs cleared up and I got out of the hospital, we kept attendant care six mornings a week, but I fell back into the comfortable pattern of depending on Gary for everything else.

He sat in front of our new computer hour after hour, intent on teaching himself how to program and me how to draw. One afternoon he coached.

"You're getting the hang of it," he said after a while. "Call me if you need any help." Before I knew it, he disappeared from sight, leaving me alone with the beast that now shared our bedroom. Its face glowed a greenish white while it hummed softly to itself. I slowly reached out with a pen clamped in my handbrace. *Let's see . . . If I move the mouse to click on this box, I can draw another straight line, right? Oops. Where did my picture go?* "Gary!"

Without his assistance—as well as his insistence—I would have gladly gone back to old-fashioned freehand drawing. But gradually, byte by reluctant byte, I learned my way around the keyboard.

While Gary pored over computer manuals, I began searching out new craft ideas in cutesy gift shops. (You know, the kind of stores that men never frequent.) My aide, Sandy, delighted in our shopping expeditions as much as I did.

The second anniversary of my accident found us planning a trip to one of our favorite stores. To keep life from getting dull, we would take her one-month-old baby along.

"You really think we can do this?" I asked.

"I don't see why not," Sandy replied with a confidence that I lacked. She loaded me into the van, then buckled the baby into her car seat. Lindsey wiggled and cooed and gave us a charming little toothless "let's go for it" grin.

When we arrived at our favorite shop, Sandy unloaded me, fastened a snuggly around her chest for Lindsey and manned the push handles on my chair. No problem!

"Look at these cute place mats," I said.

Sandy turned one over and gave a low whistle. "Can you believe the price?"

"Craft fairs!" I said.

"What?"

"I was just thinking, the design is so simple, we could stencil something like this ourselves—and I could sell them at craft fairs." *If I can make money at it, at least I'm not a total failure, right?*

"I can cut out the stencil," Sandy said.

"And I can draw a design on my computer. A simple design," I added. Three yards of canvas and a couple of paintbrushes later, we began.

"What color do you want to start with?" Sandy asked.

"Let's see, for the hearts, I think I'll go with candy-apple red." Sandy stuck one of our slender new brushes through the opening in my handbrace designed for a pen. It promptly fell out.

"Oops."

"How about if I wrap tape around the brush?" Sandy suggested.

"It's worth a try."

Twenty minutes later I decided that the fault lay with the owner/operator—not with the paintbrush. "This won't work, but I have another idea."

"So what's your idea?" Sandy asked.

"Put the paintbrush in my mouth."

She obliged. I hooked my arms around the push handles of my chair, leaned down and dabbed red paint in the cutout on the stencil.

While we worked, cars drove down the quiet street, but the wooden privacy fence kept out inquisitive stares. I kept my back turned to all the trapeze equipment gathering dust in the far corner.

Many afternoons that summer and fall found us painting place mats, Christmas ornaments and stuffed animals. By the time craft fair season rolled around in October, I had plenty of stock for my new venture.

* * *

"This looks sharp," Gary said when he finished arranging my wares.

I beamed. "With all the signs we saw around town, I bet there's a bigger turnout here than at the other three fairs. This is a dynamite location too."

My cheery table, wearing a Santa-suit red tablecloth, nestled snugly in the corner of the spacious gymnasium between the appliqued sweatshirt booth and the hand-painted dolls. A small Christmas tree, adorned with my hand-stenciled ornaments, occupied a prominent spot in the middle. To the left, I displayed handmade stationery and cards. On the right sat an old wicker chest practically bursting at the seams with stenciled teddy bears, cats and geese.

That first morning I checked out the rest of the booths and talked with other enthusiastic sellers.

"Business was kind of slow today," my Christmas candle neighbor two booths down said when we closed up shop, "but wait till tomorrow. I did this fair last year and I practically sold out on Saturday."

"Really? This is the last fair I signed up for—and I have yet to see a profit. . . ."

"Wait till tomorrow," Jan predicted with a smile. "You'll see."

The following morning, with a heightened sense of anticipation, I made sure that Gary and I arrived extra early. All day long I sat. I watched. I waited. "Where are they?" I finally asked Gary.

"Who?"

"The buyers! All those generous 'money burning a hole in my pocket' buyers that Jan told me about yesterday." I turned and stared in disbelief at Jan's empty booth. "She left already?"

We looked around the unusually quiet gymnasium. Gary verbalized my thoughts. "It looks like the sellers outnumber the buyers."

"But I barely made the lousy booth fee back!"

"You sold as much as everyone else," Gary pointed out. "It's not your fault so few people showed up."

Yes it is, a small voice taunted. *You're a failure, Little Circus Girl. So much for having faith in yourself.*

Despair replaced the light which had flickered so briefly in my eyes. I shivered as the weak flame of hope sputtered before giving up the ghost.

CHAPTER TWELVE

Looking for an Easy Way Out

I relax in the soothing water of the hot springs pool, my favorite vacation spot as a child. Slowly, I rise to a standing position. Incredibly, I begin to walk! Wonder, relief and excitement flood my being. At last I can begin to live again.

The dream faded and the reality of permanent quadriplegia hit home. Tears squeezed out from beneath my closed lids. Another detestable Sunday morning awaited me. Gary—my sole weekend help—wouldn't waken for hours. I scrunched up both eyes and peered at the clock. *Only 6:00? It figures.* A panicky, "I can't move until Gary is good and ready to get up" feeling washed over me.

And nothing will ever change.

The sight of cardboard boxes lining the hall crowded out all other thoughts. Leftovers. Unwanted, unsold crafts. How do I kill time now?

You're a failure, Little Circus Girl, a sinister voice broke into my thoughts. *You can't do anything right.*

"Are you awake?" Gary asked hours later.

I turned my head. "Yes."

He reached for the remote.

Relieved to have the mindless distraction of television, I stared at the screen with unseeing eyes, listened with unhearing ears.

Gary fixed himself a cup of coffee. I tuned out. After he got me up, I divided my time between the television set and a trashy novel, paying little attention to either.

"What do I want for dinner?" I repeated Gary's question like a parrot. "Um . . . what do we have?"

Gary opened the pantry. He detested cooking as much as I disliked eating, so he kept his culinary efforts to a minimum. Twenty minutes later we sat together at the dining room table. After my first few bites of sawdust-flavored corned beef hash and eggs my stomach revolted. Similar to dry heaves, I called them stomach spasms, for lack of a better term. They struck at random every day. When the attack subsided, I picked at the rest of the tasteless food on my plate.

"Gary, would you put me to bed when you're done eating?"

"Dizzy?" he asked.

I frowned. "It never fails—no matter what I eat."

"Why don't you make an appointment to see a doctor? Find out what's wrong and take care of the problem."

His suggestion gave my brain the jump start it needed. Relief flickered as I thought, *This is something I can change.*

A phone call the next day yielded results. My doctor referred me to a specialist, who scheduled some tests. The following week, he called back.

"Hello, Mrs. Baker? Dr. Payne here. Your tests came back negative."

"Negative?" I repeated in disbelief.

"Yes. I'm happy to give you a clean bill of health. Do you have any other questions?"

"Ah, n-no," I stammered.

"Then good-bye."

Click.

Good-bye to you too, doc. Have a nice life. I listened to the dial tone for a long time before disconnecting. *Now what?* An endless parade of empty, dizzy days stretched out before me like grains of sand in a a vast desert. The doctor had just sentenced me to life without the possibility of parole. The paralyzing venom of despair filled my heart.

"What did he say?" Gary called from the living room.

I wheeled toward him. "The tests didn't show anything wrong. As far as he's concerned, I'm just fine. He doesn't care whether I live or die."

Do I?

The question struck from nowhere, but had hovered at the edge of consciousness ever since the accident.

"I don't know how much longer I can take this," I said.

"I don't blame you." Gary's voice had a hollow, empty ring. He looked a mere shadow of his former self. His haunted, faraway gaze—the eyes of a condemned man—held no promise of a better tomorrow. No smile graced his tightly pursed lips. Laughter? A thing of the past. The weight of depression made his shoulders sag.

Lying awake that night, I thought about a support group I'd attended earlier in the week. Only one other woman had come and we'd spent the entire hour discussing the need for wheelchair accessible "jumping off" spots on high bridges. Some support!

My mind reeled back to the string of counselors and psychologists Gary and I had gone to see. We'd given up on every last one. Nobody had any answers. Nobody could tell us how to rebuild a meaningful life together. Life seemed to have no meaning at all.

I thought about the growing stack of Spinal Cord Society (SCS) newsletters on the living room table. The last three issues of SCS remained unread. I had pretty much given up on the hope of a modern-day miracle that would set my feet on high places again. The "just around the corner" cure that would allow me to wrap my fully-functioning fingers around a flybar and sail through the air with the greatest of ease wasn't ever going to happen. Few friends stopped by anymore. *What's left? Maybe I just don't know where to find help. Some people turn to religion when things get bad. . . .*

I recalled Sunday mornings growing up. The routine—wake up early, put on a dress, ride to church. The ritual—stand, sit, kneel. Kneel, sit, stand. Repeat mumbo jumbo in unison to a vague, unapproachable God. When I got home, I would stuff my dress—and God—back into the closet until the next Sunday rolled around; and the next, until I moved away from home and stopped going.

Could Mom's distant God help me now?

You never gave Him so much as the time of day, a voice hissed in my ear. *What makes you think He would want to have anything to do with you now? You're worthless, Little Circus Girl. You'd be better off dead.*

"Dead?" my shaky voice pierced the darkness.

Go ahead, do it, the voice nudged. *What have you got to lose?*

And so it came to pass that energy surfaced. Devious schemes hatched. The dam of apathy burst and dark, sinister thoughts sprang to life. Twisted ideas swirled through the dark lonely hours of the night.

The following evening I watched the news with morbid fascination. "Look at that poor guy," I said to Gary.

I watched in horror as my worst fears flickered across the screen. A young overdose victim sat slumped over in a manual wheelchair, misery written all over his face. A feeding tube protruded from his nose. A regulation hospital gown clothed his nakedness.

"The drugs he took caused total paralysis from the neck down," a reporter's voice boomed. "He cannot speak and he is unable to swallow."

I gasped. "How can he stand it? He has no control over anything. He can't operate that wheelchair. He can't eat . . . he can't even communicate!"

"On his behalf, his brother is petitioning the courts for the right to have his feeding tube disconnected."

Thank goodness.

In the days to come, I anxiously followed the drug victim's "progress." When the courts granted his request, I applauded their decision. Two weeks later my new role model died.

"Gary, I don't want to live this way any longer. Let's face it, I'll always have these eating problems and I'll always be dizzy and half-passing out."

My husband's sad-eyed gaze spoke volumes. "I understand. I see what you go through every day."

"And as long as we're together you can't work . . . so there's no future for us as a couple. And nothing will ever change!"

"I know," Gary said. "I feel worthless. Every time we see your uncle, he keeps asking when I'm going to get a job. No one seems to understand how that would affect your benefits—and that you can't be without health insurance."

"I don't see any point in sticking around." I took in a deep breath. "Will you stand behind me on this decision?"

"Yes . . . but I'm not willing to face time behind bars for helping you."

"Don't worry, I won't involve you. I'll figure something out."

The next day, Gary took me to the library. We looked through all the newspaper accounts of the overdose victim's death for details possibly not aired.

"It says here that he refused water too," I said.

"I've heard that dehydration can be painful," Gary said.

I shuddered. "Then forget that idea. I'll keep looking. I certainly don't want this to hurt."

We browsed through the card catalog, found a wealth of information and headed home with an armload of books. Burrowing down with Derrick Humphries' first "how-to" book on death—his sequel not out at that early date—gave me ideas, but I didn't have the resources to follow through.

"This one tells how a woman helped her terminally ill mother to die," I commented to Gary a few nights later. "A Dutch doctor flew to the United States at the appropriate time to 'help her mother out.' " (Living in pre-Kevorkian times, she'd had to make do with the limited killer-doctors available.)

"But that won't work for me," I continued. "I only know doctors who help people to get better—not worse. Of course there were a few who tried to annoy me to death, but there has to be an easier way than that."

A couple nights later, after his third or fourth beer, Gary said, "I'll help you do it."

I looked up. "But I don't want you to get in trouble because of—"

"I won't. I'm going to join you."

"Oh. OK." So keenly wrapped up in my own ravaged emotions, I didn't even question Gary's decision.

We took off in our little car and headed in the general direction of the mountains. Once we found a secluded spot to park, Gary pulled out the remainder of his six-pack.

"Stan knows he gets the cat," I said.

"And the computer goes to Ray," Gary added.

"I'm glad I gave my quilt to my cousin, Rob. I put an awful lot of work into it."

We lapsed into silence.

I looked over at Gary. "Well, I guess that's that."

He looked back. "Then this is it. Are you ready?"

I felt strangely exhilarated. "More than ready."

Gary gave me a sloppy beer-breath kiss, grabbed the vacuum cleaner hose and the duct tape and stepped outside. The darkness swallowed him. I could hear him fumbling around. Finally, he threaded the hose through a back window, stumbled back in and turned on the engine. We looked at each other one last time. I closed my eyes and inhaled deeply. But a few minutes later, we realized that something wasn't working right. Gary got out to investigate. The skimpy hose had melted in two.

With nothing left to do and suddenly very thirsty, we turned around and headed home.

Now what?

Gary took me back to the library. A book on fasting caught my eye. I read with growing interest, and a few days later an idea formed.

"I think I've got it," I said.

Gary looked up from his book. "Got what?"

"My exit plan—my *final* exit plan. A fast. A fast unto death. I'll stop eating, but I'll keep drinking water. Three—four weeks tops—I'll be history." I took in a deep breath. "You're going to keep eating when I stop, aren't you?"

"Yes."

In bed that night, I breathed a sigh of relief.

You can do it, Little Circus Girl, the twisted thought entered. *Go for it. I'll help you get free. Go for it.*

◆◆◆◆◆◆

"Why would I want to tell my parents?" I asked Gary the following morning.

"Think about it," he said. "You talk to them or see them at least once a week. Sooner or later they'll find out and they could make you stop. What if they called the police—"

"Do you really think they'd do that?"

"I don't know. But do you want to take the chance?"

"Well, no, but . . ." Reluctantly, I dialed my parents' number and asked them to come over. The four of us sat out in the sun room. When I announced the plan, my mother's face turned chalky-white.

"How can you consider such a thing, honey?"

"It beats the alternative," I said, staring out the dirty window. "I'm sick of living this way—and nothing's ever going to change."

My dad didn't say anything but looked like he might cry any minute. By the time they left, I knew that I could count on my parents to not interfere.

"That wasn't as hard as I thought," I said to Gary. "I think I'll also tell Bruce . . . and maybe Rob—but that's it. They're about the only people we still see . . . and they won't have much to say about it. They both look at this wheelchair as a fate worse than death."

With "good-byes" out of the way, Day Number One finally dawned. No point gettin' out of bed anymore. Just tune out and drift away. Take a swig of water now and then, but don't eat. *No, don't eat,* the voice echoed.

Nothing mattered. Nothing expected of me, nothing delivered. Just coasting to the finish line. *You got it made, Little Circus Girl.* Like a lullaby, the voice comforted, calmed, soothed my jagged nerves.

My limited horizontal world included a comfortable waterbed, a large television set atop the dresser and a porcelain lamp that had trooped 15,000 miles with Gary and me.

Four weeks later, "Gilligan's Island" and "I Love Lucy" turned as stale as my attitude. Gary changed the channel for me one day and left the room before the commercial had ended. I paid little attention until a TV evangelist pointed his bony finger at me and shouted, "God loves you!"

God doesn't even know me! my mind screamed.

"God only wants what's best for you!" the booming voice continued.

Yeah, right.

Hang in there, death whispered. *It won't be long now.*

On day number forty-two, my cousin visited. "Gee, Vickie, I can't believe how good you look."

How good I look? Rob's words echoed through the house, bounced off the walls, rolled around in my head and settled in my throat, hard to swallow. I longed for the blessed release that only death could bring.

Like an unwanted intruder, pain stalked into my rosy plans and fogged my thinking. Entire trains of thought derailed. We got our hands on a little stash of pain pills. Powerful miracles dressed up in tiny, round packages—blockbusters that knocked me out for hours. Good. I rationed them ever so cautiously—it never occurred to me to overdose on them. Never occurred to me at all.

Sleep . . . wake up . . . sip water . . . another magic pill and back to never-never land. The voice in my head nudged, deceived. *Soon you'll be free, Little Circus Girl. Free.* I drifted in and out. Gently, like bobbing in the water at the hot-springs pool.

Suddenly, the pills stopped working. Jagged, shooting pains racked my body. Words and thoughts got all snarled up together as they spewed out of my mouth. Whining, whimpering, I heard myself begging for help. "Let's use the other vacuum cleaner hose Gary—the metal one we bought at the thrift store. Let's use it now!"

Did I think those words or actually say them? Must have said them. Strong arms picked me up, blanket and all. Cool air brushed my furrowed brow. Cloudy, damp night. Gary gently placed me on a comfortable couch. The van door slammed shut and a quiet hush descended. Visualizing the end, I hungered for the exhaust fumes.

Death—so greatly welcomed. The end—never occurred. The relief—never came. *Instead, the police came and brought me here.*

I stared at the shabby walls of the darkened room with disgust. *Held hostage. But where? Can't think straight.* My malnourished mind drew a blank. Nothing looked familiar. I didn't recognize anyone in the other beds. I lay all alone in a room full of strangers.

PART FOUR

Happy
to Be Alive

CHAPTER THIRTEEN

This Present Reality

◆—◆—◆—◆—◆

*L*ike an astronaut just back from outer space, my mind touched down in the here-and-now. *Where am I?*

I looked around the empty room in amazement while pieces of the recent past cut through the confusion. *Suicide attempt failed . . . police came . . . Gary was locked up . . . I'm on a seventy-two hour hold . . . beds—weren't there other beds in here?*

Just then a young man with dark, curly hair and a friendly smile glided through the door. "Hi. My name is Zac. I'll be your nurse today."

Zac talked on. My sluggish mind struggled to keep up.

"I'm glad to see you're finally out of intensive care."

"Intensive care?"

"Don't you remember? You got a bladder infection and you've been in the intensive care unit for the past five days. . . ."

Five days? I was supposed to be out of here in three.

"What . . . what happened?"

"You had urosepsis. The bacteria from the bladder infection got into your bloodstream. . . ."

Zac's words only made me more confused. I shook my head trying to clear my vision which was also foggy. Keeping one eye closed, I squinted. "Would you mind standing on the other side of the bed?"

"Sure," he said. "Why?"

"When I turn my head to the left, I see about six of you; but that doesn't happen when I look straight ahead or to the right."

He jotted something down and walked to the other side.

"How much longer do I have to be here?" I blurted.

"You'll have to ask your doctor," Zac said, turning very businesslike.

My mind wandered.

"Vickie, do you feel like hurting yourself?"

"Huh? . . . Um, no."

"Do you feel like hurting other people?"

"No."

"Do you drink alcohol? Take street drugs?"

"No."

Before leaving, Zac turned me. Since he'd worked with quads at Craig, he knew the proper way to position me to prevent pressure sores.

Exhausted, I dozed until an aide brought in a lunch tray and stayed to feed me.

"I'll check on you later," she said when I finished.

Shortly after she carried away the tray, my bowels let loose again. I hit the call switch. *Why is this happening?*

Once my nurse cleaned me up, I dozed, but awakened sometime later when a "white-coat" approached. The hair on the back of my neck bristled. There was something familiar about that unshaven face, that cold, indifferent stare. When he spoke, déjà vu struck. I recognized the same expression on Dr. Gloom's stern face that I'd seen in the ER when the paramedics brought me in. He asked about my vision and chronic diarrhea, then started in with the "is she in touch with reality" questions.

"What year is it?"

"1987."

"What month is it?"

"August . . . I think."

After I'd gone through the "now count backward from 100 by sevens" part, a lengthy pause jerked me back to the present.

"I'm sorry. What did you say?"

"How was your childhood?"

"Um . . . fine . . . except that when I was four, my only brother, Woody, died. The family was crossing the street. He dropped his toy and when he ran back for it, he was hit. . . ."

Suddenly, the burlap sack buried deep in my heart—the one stuffed with twenty-eight-years-worth of smoldering emotions—burst into flames. Grief, too big for a four-year-old to express, washed over me as if Woody's accident had happened yesterday.

Questions never before voiced slashed through the chaos. But directed to whom? To God? *If God exists, why did He let Woody die? Why did my accident have to happen? Why, God? Why?*

The debate raged on for days. I recall crying a great deal of the time after my meetings with Dr. Gloom. While I poured out my grief, his icy demeanor never changed. He listened to my nonstop chatter on a daily basis, yet rarely said a word—encouraging or otherwise. All the while, sinister thoughts assaulted my mind. *You're nothing, Little Circus Girl. Nothing. Why would God care about you?*

❖❖❖❖❖❖

Goose bumps raised on my arms and my face felt hot. A dull, pounding ache stormed into my head. My eyes opened wide with fear. Those of us living with quadriplegia heed the warning signs of autonomic dysreflexia. From my spinal cord injury handbook and the laminated card I carried in my wallet, I knew that I needed help right away.

I tapped the call device.

What's causing it? My catheter's draining, isn't it? Thank goodness I have Zac tonight. He'll know what to do.

Moments later, a nurse I'd never seen before appeared. "What do you need, Vickie?"

"Where's Zac?"

"He went home sick."

I drew in a deep breath. Using my very best "I've been a quad for over three years so I know what I'm talking about" tone of voice I explained the problem, highlighting the causes as well as the symptoms. My eyes threatened to bug out of my head as internal pressure mounted.

"Dysreflexia?" she questioned, a doubtful look on her face.

She doesn't believe me!

I raced on. "I realize few people on this floor know much about spinal cord injury. Will you please call my doctor at Craig? I can't figure out what's causing it—"

She scowled. "Can't this wait till morning?"

"No! Dysreflexia does not go away until you treat the problem."

She stomped toward the door. "I'll be back."

The overhead lights glared. My temperature rose and my head throbbed.

Finally, the nurse marched back in with the on-call doctor in tow who looked even less pleased with my 3:00 a.m. nuisance call.

Haughty eyes bore into me. "Now then, what seems to be the problem?"

I explained.

After staring down at me for what seemed like hours, Dr. "High 'n' Mighty" spoke very slowly, as if trying to pacify a six-year-old. "Now, dearie..."

My breath caught in my throat. *Dearie?*

"Don't you think this was caused by the stresses of the past few days?"

"No!" I practically shouted. By now, sweat rolled off my forehead. Through clenched teeth I repeated, "Dysreflexia is caused by a plugged catheter, a bowel problem, lying on a sharp object below the level of sensation, a broken bone or an ingrown toenail."

Hours later, the symptoms mysteriously vanished on their own, baffling me even more, but the following morning I learned that the ICU staff had changed my catheter and my body couldn't tolerate this type. When my nurse discovered that the hospital did not carry the kind I needed, my mind went to work. I explained the problem to Dr. Gloom when he appeared.

"And you say you have some extra silicone catheters at home?" he asked.

I nodded. "Would it be OK if I ask someone to bring in a few? I need to get this one changed as soon as possible and I'd like to keep a couple in my room in case it plugs up again."

His typically rigid expression softened a bit. "Yes, that will be fine. Your nurse can make the call for you. I'll send her in."

A few hours later my mom arrived bearing a large grocery sack. "Hi, baby. Daddy's parking the car." She set the bag down and started pulling stuff out. "I brought three catheters and trays."

"Good. Did you bring my spinal cord injury handbook and make some copies?"

"Yes. But why—"

"Because I need to educate these people about dysreflexia. No one who works here—except for Zac—knows a thing about spinal cord injury. I'm not safe here. I want to transfer to Swedish."

"Now, honey, don't you think you're exaggerating? Your doctor only wants what's best for you. He says it's important for you to be here right now."

My voice rose an octave. "Mom, I could have died last night! My catheter wouldn't drain and. . . ."

Mom chose to ignore my ranting and raving, as did my father who had just walked in and stood silently by her side.

"Your doctor seems like a very nice man," Mom continued.

Yes, Mother.

◆◆◆◆◆◆

The next afternoon, somewhere between the diarrhea and the lonely boredom, a familiar figure approached.

"Hello, Vickie."

I looked up in amazement. *Am I hallucinating again? How can this be? He lives over 2,000 miles away.*

"Wh-what are you doing here? When—"

"I just flew in last night. I'm staying at a motel not too far from here," my father-in-law stated matter-of-factly, as if his son's predicament didn't seem the least bit odd.

I'd never spent much time around him when Gary and I breezed through Delaware on our way to and from shows, and now I felt awkward. No words came, but my father-in-law talked on, oblivious to my silence.

"Gary's doing OK. He spent five days in the hospital's jail ward, then he was moved to the city jail last week. They're releasing him tomorrow."

"Tomorrow?"

"I'll pick him up and take him to your house," he continued, "so I imagine he'll come to see you sometime in the afternoon."

Tomorrow afternoon!

"I'm flying out the day after tomorrow. I'll stop in again before I go."

I watched him leave, my mind a jumble of emotions. *Will Gary want to see me? How's he going to feel?*

After dinner that night one of my favorite aides stopped by. "Would you like to meet a new patient on the floor, Vickie?"

"Are you serious? Sure!"

Moments later, a tall, husky-looking man about my age trudged through the door wearing one of those lovely one-size-fits-all hospital gowns. With one hand, he pushed an IV pole. With the other, he held the gap closed in back.

"Hi, I'm Matt." He plopped into a chair in the corner.

"I'm Vickie. Is this your first night here?"

"Yeah. I was in ICU last night."

I smiled. "Join the club. . . ."

Three hours later, Matt shuffled back out the door.

The next morning I heard a tap. "Come in," I said, wondering who in the world would knock.

Matt strolled into the room carrying an old guitar. "Lynn found this in one of the storage closets and lent it to me." With IV bottle still in tow, my new friend began to strum and sing.

I closed my eyes and let his deep baritone voice carry me away. "You can really play! Do you sing and play professionally?"

Matt looked startled. "No, I'm not good enough—"

"Who says? *I'd* pay to hear you."

Matt set the battered old instrument down and stared at me in genuine amazement. "You would?"

"Absolutely. I'll be your first customer."

❖❖❖❖❖

Sawdust filled my mouth when Gary walked through the door. He looked tired and his pale face appeared gaunt. A lifetime's worth of changes had taken place since I'd landed here. He walked over to my bed and kissed me. I felt shy. We looked at each other for a moment, then both started talking at once. Gary had a faraway look in his eyes, as if not quite in sync with reality.

"It's good to see you," he said.

"I'm glad you're out. How was it?"

"Pretty bad. They treated everyone like we'd already been found guilty. I looked like a bum when they took me to see the judge." Gary began to pace back and forth. "I had on the same T-shirt and shorts that I wore that night and I had no way to shave. . . ." His voice trailed off.

Two aides popped in to take my vital signs, so Gary went outside for a cigarette. When he returned, he continued with his tale.

"I never slept very well . . . and no one would ever tell me what time it was. There were no windows. . . ."

Half an hour later, Gary looked at his watch. "I want to stay longer, but I'm beat. I'll come back tomorrow."

When he returned the following evening, he looked more rested. His cheeks had a little color. He saw me lying down. "Why are you still in bed? Haven't you gotten up in a chair yet?"

"No. But there's no point until I stop having the runs. Everything I eat goes right through me."

"What have you been eating?"

"Whatever I want—bacon, eggs, hamburgers. And it tastes good! I actually look forward to eating!"

Gary wrote something down.

My mind seemed to race along faster than I could get the words out, yet when visiting hours ended an hour's worth of conversation later, I had no idea what we'd talked about.

Gary stood up. "Remember that book about fasting? Do you recall what it said about how to break the fast?"

"No . . . do you think that's why I'm having this problem?"

"Could be. I'll stop by the library in the morning and see if I can find the book."

We said hasty good-byes since a grim-faced nurse arrived armed with a fresh gown and a container to empty my drainage-bag.

Just then, a familiar face peeked through the doorway.

"Bruce! Come in!"

"Visiting hours are over for the day," the nurse shot out.

My smile disappeared. "Sorry, Bruce."

I heard snatches of Gary's brief conversation with him outside my door.

"Off the wall statements . . . Said she absolutely must speak with Alex from the TV show 'Taxi.' Hallucinations. . . . Need to find out the proper way to break the fast. Yes, she's in serious danger. . . ."

The voices faded.

What's wrong with me? I'm so confused. My mixed-up mind spun in circles all night. Sleep finally caught up with me ten minutes before the breakfast tray arrived.

That afternoon Gary returned bearing a book. He skimmed the chapter on fasting and read, "It is possible to do extreme or even mortal damage by breaking the fast incorrectly. . . . You need to start by drinking apricot juice and eating plain yogurt."

A few pages farther, Gary looked up. "Do you know what kind of vitamins they're giving you?"

"Vitamins? I'm not taking any vitamins."

With a frown, Gary wrote himself a note. "I'll start bringing you vitamins. And I can bring in the juice and the yogurt—"

"Say," I interrupted, my mind a thousand miles away. "Did I tell you what 'Taxi' was about last night? I actually laughed out loud! Remember the one where they all go out and get different jobs? Alex was a riot. . . ."

CHAPTER FOURTEEN

Maybe God
Does Exist

❖━━◆━━◆━━◆━━❖

Unannounced, the pair casually strolled into my room.

"We're here to take you down to physical therapy," the tall, dark-haired one said. "Can you be ready in five minutes?"

His partner, sporting a mouth full of braces, pushed a reclining wheelchair.

"Physical therapy? Well, no . . . I can't. I'm not dressed and my nurse isn't on the floor."

The two turned and fled without another word. I felt like a freak in a sideshow. *And that's never going to change!* my mind screamed.

Moments later I heard the *click-clack* of footsteps outside my door.

"Ms. Baker?"

I looked up.

A large woman with a serious frown marched through the door. "Why did you refuse physical therapy?"

"Huh?"

"You should have been ready when the orderlies arrived. They work on a tight schedule."

"But—"

"There's simply no excuse for this type of behavior. Don't you want to get stronger so you can go home?"

"Yes, but I—"

"This had better not happen tomorrow."

With that, the woman spun around and self-righteously clattered back out the door, heels smoking. My tears would not stop.

An hour later Gary arrived with his eyes downcast and shoulders slumped, a common occurance since his release from city jail the week before. We still tap-danced around the ominous topic of the future, but the pettiness of the daily grind seemed to occupy my every waking hour.

"What's wrong?" Gary asked.

Between sobs, my story spilled out. "It's not fair!" I wailed. "It's not my fault I wasn't ready. I can't dress myself."

Gary found out that my doctor had scheduled me to go down for physical therapy three times a week but had forgotten to inform the staff.

Late that night, wide awake, I stared out at the city lights—my only glimpse of freedom. But what kind of freedom? I still remained paralyzed—and I still had no desire to live.

Oh, God. God? What did He have to do with anything? He played no role in my life. I'd never had time for Him, what with deadlines to meet, costumes to design and acts to polish. But now the glitter and glamour of center ring had turned into nothing more than a bittersweet memory. Life had backed me into a corner. I had time on my gimpy hands, nothing to do and no control over anything.

God, I'm trapped. There's no way out. A realization swept over me like a tidal wave—I couldn't even kill myself right! I had no place left to run, nowhere left to turn.

God, I need help! I can't handle everything by myself anymore.

That night, for the first time since my arrival, I fell into a deep, restful sleep. When my eyes opened, I peered around the room, dumbfounded. Daylight. I had slept through the entire night! For the first time since my arrival, I felt well rested.

Yesterday's encounter with the goddess of physical therapy no longer provoked tears. *Let the staff deal with my schedule. If I'm supposed to be ready for PT by 1:00, that's their problem.*

Sometime later, my nurse popped in to reposition me—without my usual reminder call.

At 12:30, Gary walked through the door with the cushion from my wheelchair at home, a pair of shorts and a couple of T-shirts.

"I'll get you dressed," he said.

"Thanks. This is a nice surprise. I didn't expect to see you so early."

A few minutes later the nurse materialized with a legbag. "We'll make sure you're ready on time today."

She had just finished strapping it to my leg when the same two orderlies arrived, pushing their bulky blue chariot.

"Ready?" one asked.

I smiled. "Yes."

"She needs to sit on this cushion," Gary said, placing it on the seat of the recliner.

The two of them gently lifted me up and set me in the chair. My feet promptly slid off the footrests, but Gary solved the problem by taping a pad behind my ankles. Our physical therapy party set off.

"This is the dayroom," Gary said when we cleared the doorway.

Eagerly, I took it in. "It looks like a regular living room!"

Half the floor space was carpeted. I saw a faded brown couch and matching easy chair and a coffee table buried beneath stacks of magazines. A giant lamp gave the room a homey touch.

"That's where the other residents eat," Gary said pointing to the other half of the dayroom that sported small, wooden tables, padded chairs and a pool table. "Once you're spending more time up, you can join them for meals."

"Good. I'm tired of doing solitary."

After I was signed out at the nurses' station, an orderly pushed my chair through the doorway that led off the ward. My heartbeat quickened.

When we arrived at the miniature therapy room, a woman bustled over. "Hi. I'm Jackie," she said. "You must be Vickie." She turned. "Are you Vickie's husband?"

"Yes," Gary said, introducing himself.

Jackie maneuvered the chair alongside one of the two raised exercise tables and transferred me. We went through some of the same exercises I'd done at Craig. Twenty minutes later she had me back in the chair.

I turned to Gary. "I'm exhausted! That's more work than I've done in the last two months combined!"

"But it's a start," he pointed out.

Just then, a huge yawn escaped me.

"It looks like you could do with a nap," Gary said. "I'll come back after dinner." I watched him leave.

Someday, I'll leave with him.

"Ready?"

I looked up to see my two young escorts. "As soon as Jackie finishes with her notes."

Shortly, Jackie emerged from her office, handed my chart to one of the orderlies and we took off. I hoped I wouldn't fall asleep on the way. I didn't, but as soon as my head touched down on the pillow, I nodded off.

After dinner I puzzled over the day's events. All day long it had felt like someone else ran the show. Not only did everything happen according to plan, but the lump in my throat—the "oh my God what am I gonna do" feeling—had virtually disappeared.

But this doesn't make sense, I argued with my-self. *Nothing has changed!*

Baffled, I idly looked down at my right arm, resting on top of the sheet. My palm faced up. *Move, hand.* To my astonishment, the limp hand slowly lifted up and flipped over. *Good grief, am I seeing things?* Scarcely daring to breathe, I willed my hand to turn over again and again.

I wonder if I'll get anything else back? My thoughts ran wild. *Is it possible that I might even walk out of here? Climb back onto a trapeze?* By the time Gary walked through the door, I had us back on the road six states away.

"Gary, there's something I want to show you! Watch my hand." Once again, the magic of move-ment occurred, just like before. I looked over ex-pectantly, but there was no response—not even a raised eyebrow. I did it again. Still nothing.

"Gary, we both know I've never been able to do this!"

He just grunted. When I looked into his eyes, I read a mixture of sadness and . . . what? Confu-sion? Despair? As if blinded by a blanket of fog, he gave me a funny look. I didn't understand, but I didn't bring it up again.

The next day after lunch Gary and my parents and I met with Dr. Gloom in his office for a con-ference. I showed them the new movement in my wrist, but again, it sparked little interest.

In bed that night, my excitement mounted while I flipped my wrist over again and again.

God . . . are You behind this? I mean, medically speaking, this isn't supposed to happen. Is this an answer to my prayer? I've heard religious people say that nothing is impossible for You. Can You . . . cure me?

For the first time since the craft fairs, a sense of calm filled my heart. Before drifting off, a new thought entered my mind. *Do not be afraid, Vickie. This is a new beginning.*

<hr />

In the stillness of dawn, I awoke with a feeling of anticipation and wiggled my right arm out from under the blanket.

Move, hand.

Nothing.

Come on, move!

My arm remained as lifeless as a corpse. Self doubts silently surfaced.

Did I just imagine this whole thing? Is it all one big hallucination? It can't be . . . can it? I saw it with my own two eyes. . . . Baffled, I stared at the limp appendage.

The new movement never did reappear and everyone's ho-hum reaction still remains a mystery to me. I finally tucked the incident away in my mind as a miracle meant just for me, but the sense of peace I'd felt the night before was immediately shot down by the evil voice. *You call this a miracle? Where's your God now, Little Circus Girl?*

I don't know. . . .

Just then my nurse breezed through the door. "Vickie, we need to get you out of this room so you can start having some fun."

Fun?

Jody chattered on. "What did you do for fun?"

"You mean since the accident? Um . . . I don't remember."

"You don't have PT today," she continued, "but I have time later on to get you dressed if you want to get up."

"Yes. Thank you!"

After she left, her question continued to haunt me. *What* did *I used to do for fun?* I still hadn't come up with an answer when Gary walked through the door. The smile on his usually serious face made me do a double take.

"Do you want to go outside tonight?"

"Outside? You mean outside this building?"

"Yes."

"Can I do that? Have you cleared it with the 'gestapo'?"

"Your nurse was the one who suggested it. She told me she'd get you up later if I help with the transfer. I want to spend some time at the library this afternoon, but I'll come back after dinner and get you up."

"I can't wait!"

<hr />

That evening, with Gary manning the push handles, we silently glided over to the nurses' station to sign out before joining a small band of residents huddled around the elevators. Almost everyone clutched cigarettes and lighters, anxious to get outside for their last smoke of the day. No one else used a wheelchair.

Am I the only gimp who's ever lost it?

"OK, we can go now," said an unfamiliar nurse who joined us.

The elevator finally opened its doors and we all crowded in. Emerging on the first floor, we hurried through the gigantic lobby. The noise level intensified, with people scurrying every which way. My heart beat faster. At the main entrance, two automatic doors sprang open.

Freedom!

Under the covered front entrance, Gary positioned my chair close to a bench, put the brakes on and parked himself downwind with a cigarette.

"This is heavenly," I murmured. "The only thing missing is the storm."

Gary looked puzzled. "Storm?"

"Yeah. I love the smell of rain and the feel of wind in my face because it means I'm outside and not cooped up in some hot, stuffy hospital room. The louder the storm the better."

As if on cue, a tremendous clap of thunder practically shook the ground beneath my chair.

Gary chuckled. "Need anything else?"

I returned his smile. "No."

The wind picked up and soon large raindrops pelted the grass next to the cement walkway, while jagged flashes of lightning tore through the inky sky. The smell of wet earth mixed with the fragrance of sweet alyssum and geraniums. Awed by the storm's dramatic display, I thought *Surely God has to be real . . . doesn't He?*

As suddenly as it blew in, the storm ceased. Looking toward the street, I spotted someone I'd met at Craig heading our way.

"Look, Gary."

My husband turned. "Hi, Dale. It's good to see you!"

Our friend motored toward us in her power chair.

I reached down. "Hi, Percy! Do you remember me?"

Her German Shepherd planted a big wet doggy kiss on the back of my hand and politely wagged her tail.

All too soon, a muffled announcement from inside the hospital signaled the end of freedom.

"I have something for you, Vickie," Dale said. She turned. "Gary, there's a paper bag in my backpack. Will you pull it out and open it?"

He extracted the contents—a tiny cassette player, earphones and an unlabeled cassette.

"What's on the tape?" I asked.

Dale hesitated. "It's a . . . mystery tape. Let me know how you like it."

"Gee, thanks, Dale."

While I watched her motor toward the parking lot, I wondered why I had set my mind against getting a chair like hers. I distinctly remembered telling a counselor that I would feel like a failure if

I went to a power chair, but I couldn't remember why.

As if reading my mind, Gary said, "Pretty neat chair she has."

"Yeah. Hers reclines. If I had a power chair, I'd want mine to recline, too."

Reluctantly we headed in the opposite direction and in no time arrived back on the ward.

"I'll put your nightgown on before I go because I want to check your skin," Gary said after he transferred me.

"See anything?" I asked when he rolled me on my side.

"The skin by your right pelvic bone is pink."

"But I was only up for forty-five minutes!"

"You've been in bed all summer," Gary reminded me. "You need to build up your time slowly—and remember to ask someone to give you weight shifts when I'm not around."

"I will," I promised. "The last thing I need is a pressure sore."

"Need anything before I go?"

"Yes. Will you give me the headphones and turn on Dale's tape?"

Gary popped the tape into the tiny machine. After a hasty discussion about when he would come back tomorrow, he slipped the headphones over my ears and hit "play."

In the semidarkened room, I listened to Dale's tape over and over. This became a ritual in the many long nights to come. "On Eagle's Wings" became my favorite. The song seemed to reach down into my very soul, and gradually a sliver of hope squeezed in, paralyzed limbs and all. The words proclaimed that God would raise me up on eagle's wings and hold me in the palm of His hand. Consciously tuning out the accusing voice chattering away in my head, I gave myself permission to enjoy the comfort these words brought.

God, I'm still paralyzed, and my hand hasn't moved anymore . . . but the future doesn't look quite as bleak. Why?

Making Plans

———◆—◆—◆—◆—◆———

"Vickie, I have some free time this morning. Would you like to get up and have a tour?"

"You'd go to all that trouble for me?"

My nurse, Hope, smiled. "It's not that much trouble. You've been here for over three weeks. It's time you started getting out of this room now that you can spend more time up in the chair."

"OK, sure," I agreed. "Where are we going?"

"You'll see."

Forty-five minutes later, we set off.

"Have you met many of the other residents on the floor?"

"Only a few."

We headed out to the dayroom. Two young men, intent on a game of pool, stood with their backs toward us.

161

"You've met Matt, haven't you?" Hope asked.
"Yes."

At the sound of our voices, both men turned.
Matt looked surprised. "You're up!"

I smiled.

"Vickie, this is my roomie, Carlos," Matt said.

After introductions, Hope wheeled me toward the back room where a few residents sat watching a game show. I could have easily gabbed all day if Hope hadn't interrupted.

"Would you like to go outside?"

"Yes! I'll take sunshine and fresh air over a hospital ward any day."

We headed for the elevator.

"Hope, why don't I see visitors on the floor when I'm up? My parents and Gary come to see me almost every day and my friends are in and out a lot, but I never see anyone else getting visitors."

"A lot of the patients lead fairly isolated lives. Quite a few will go to a shelter when they leave."

"A shelter? Why?"

"No money, no job, no family or friends to help them get back on their feet. There used to be more support from government agencies."

And I thought I had it rough.

Hope parked my chair by a tree near the front entrance.

I basked in the warmth. "Whenever I'm doing time in a hospital," I confided, "the real healing seems to start when I get to go outside—even if it's just for a little while."

Hope looked at her watch. "That's good, because I need to get back in a few minutes."

I drew in a deep breath and looked around the spacious grounds. Other patients relaxed nearby. Two squirrels playing tag disappeared up a tree.

Hope released my brakes. "We have time for one more stop."

Back inside the elevator, she punched "three." On the third floor, we cruised down a long corridor. "This is the chapel."

When we cleared the doorway, I stared in awe. A quiet hush surrounded us. Red carpet, stained glass and polished pews replaced the harsh institutional sting of cold tile floors, blaring announcements and the ever-present god-docs.

"Listen!" I said, glorying in the sense of calmness that washed over me.

Hope gave me a puzzled look. "I don't hear anything."

"Exactly!"

Moments later when my private tour ended, I vowed to escape to the chapel as often as possible.

"Do you want to stay up until therapy and eat out here?" Hope asked.

"That sounds great!"

When I lay down after physical therapy that afternoon, I slept clear until dinnertime. Gary arrived around 7:00.

My doctor had upgraded me to "B" status, so we took the elevator down all by ourselves. When we slipped outside, I recognized quite a few fellow residents sitting by the entrance. We parked farther away.

"Gary, I met some of the other people on the floor this morning. The problems they face . . . I never realized how lucky I am."

Gary gave me a questioning look.

"They might be able-bodied, but a lot of them have worse problems than mine. If someone doesn't have outside support, they're in trouble. . . . You know, I'd like to do something to help other people. Maybe I could do some volunteer work when I get out."

"Why don't you go back to school?" Gary suggested. "Go into social work."

My mouth dropped open. "Me? But I can't—"

"If you had a chair like Dale's, you could get around campus by yourself all day."

◆──◆──◆──◆──◆

The more I thought about Gary's idea, the more I liked it. *I could do something that would make a difference. What a novel idea!*

The next day after dinner, a problem I'd experienced the week before—dysreflexia—struck full force, making my head pound. Fortunately, Gary arrived at the same time as the on-call doctor. The doctor left the room for a minute and Gary got my catheter unplugged. When the doctor returned I told him how Gary had solved the problem.

He looked a bit confused.

"That's nice," he finally conceded. "I'm going to take a blood sample."

My disbelief bubbled to the surface. *Drawing blood has nothing to do with dysreflexia!* my indignant mind screamed. In the end, too tired to argue, I meekly held out my arm for a useless blood test. *Where's your God now, Little Circus Girl?*

Good question. I had no answer as confusion and doubt battled for control of my ragged emotions.

"We need to get you out of here," Gary said after the doctor left. "You're safer at home."

"I'll say. He didn't have the faintest idea what dysreflexia was. Heaven forbid he should admit to such a crime. Better to kill off the patient—"

What if Gary hadn't come in tonight? The thought hit me like a fist as Jackson, a quad I'd met during rehab, popped into my mind. Poor guy. One night after he'd gotten out, his catheter plugged up. Help didn't arrive soon enough and he stroked out and died. Died! At the age of thirty-two! My present age. . . . Goose bumps shivered down my arms.

Sitting outside that evening, Gary and I continued our discussion.

"Yesterday your nurse asked me why you're still here," Gary said. "I told her that I don't know. Do you?"

"Well, no, now that the diarrhea is pretty much cleared up. But I'll sure find out tomorrow."

◆━◆━◆━◆━◆

"I can't leave," I wailed when Gary arrived the next evening. "The doctor kept telling me he doesn't see that anything has changed at home. It felt like I was talking to a parrot!"

"Did you tell him about your plans?"

"Yeah, and he wanted to know what I'm going to do forty-eight months down the road, after I've gotten my degree and I'm working when that state program I'm going to have to apply for—the Plan for Achieving Self-Support (PASS)—and my benefits—run out!

"I'd be better off in jail. At least there I'd have a release date—and maybe the guards wouldn't play quite as many mind games.

"You know what will happen next, don't you? He'll talk to my mom, like he did that time I wanted to transfer to Swedish. He'll tell her how much I need his expert care—"

"Expert care?" Gary asked. "Whenever I see him in the hallway he ignores me and looks the other way. Do you find it helpful talking to him?"

"Not particularly. I'm usually in tears by the time he leaves."

The next morning, Dr. Gloom surprised me. After my "I want to go home" greeting and his baffling "I don't see that anything has changed at home" answer, he offered me an eight-hour parole.

I stared in disbelief. "A pass? For all day Saturday?"

"You would need to be back by 5:00."

"I can live with that."

At 6:00 a.m. Saturday morning I awoke, excited as a child on Christmas morning. An entire day of freedom stretched out before me. A few hours later, the big moment arrived when Gary walked through the door. A warm, peaceful September morning graced our departure.

"Tortilla Flats for lunch?"

I smiled. "Where else?"

After a wonderful meal, Gary pulled up in front of the townhouse. Our hasty midnight departure four weeks earlier seemed a lifetime ago.

When Gary wheeled me through the front door, Punkin rubbed against his leg and sniffed at the chair. "Here you go, Punk." He scooped up the cat and set him on my lap.

"Hi, Sweet Stuff," I murmured, stroking his long fur.

Punkin gave me an accusatory look, jumped down and pranced away, pointedly ignoring me.

We both laughed.

"Such an affectionate creature," I said.

"He'll come around once you're home for good."

"Yeah, right," I grumbled.

Gary pushed the bulky hospital chair out to the patio and pulled out a lawn chair for himself. The sunshine's soothing warmth felt good on my face. Punkin stalked grasshoppers in the lush grass while we talked.

"My court date is next week," Gary said. "I want you to come with me."

"I'd like to. I shouldn't have any trouble getting a pass."

"I have to be there at 9:00," Gary continued, "so I'll come in early to get you dressed."

"What happens at a preliminary hearing?"

"The judge will set a date for a formal plea and decide if a public defender will be assigned. It shouldn't take very long—we won't discuss my part in your suicide attempt until the official hearing."

I glanced at my watch. "Yikes! It's almost time to go back." The thought brought tears to my eyes.

Rolling through the double doors leading to the psych ward felt like a death sentence. Gary didn't plan to come in the next day, so I stayed in bed. A few circus fliers from the Y visited in the afternoon and Matt stopped by after dinner.

"My nurse asked me to play my guitar at the community meeting tonight."

"Great! Let me know how it goes."

Matt frowned. "Can't you come?"

"I doubt it. There aren't any orderlies on the floor to get me in my chair and Gary's not coming in."

Just then my nurse walked through the door.

Matt turned to her. "Everyone else gets to go to these meetings except for Vickie—and she's been here for over a month. Can't she come tonight?"

To my shock, Toni smiled and said, "I think that can be arranged. Janie can help me with the transfer."

At 9:00 p.m. sharp, Toni wheeled me to my first group meeting. I recognized most of the other residents, noted the conspicuous absence of doctors and enjoyed the relaxed, easygoing atmosphere. Toni wheeled me toward two empty chairs in the circle, moved one out of the way and sat down. She held my glass of juice up for me to take a sip.

When everyone found a seat, Sherri, the ward's psychologist, spoke. "Matt is going to play for us tonight."

I soon found myself swaying in time to the music until he sang "On the Road Again." When the song ended, Sherri turned toward me.

"What's wrong?"

Embarrassed by my tears, I stared at the floor. "It . . . it's just that it brings back old memories," I said. "Whenever Gary and I left town, we'd pop Willie Nelson into the tape deck . . . but now we won't be going back on the road again. That part of my life is over." I took in a deep breath. "Now it's time to move on."

In bed that night I realized that I had finally admitted it. *I will never perform again. The casting act is dead. The balancing act does not exist anymore. The perch act is history.* All alone, my tears flowed freely. Would the truth ever stop hurting so much?

❖❖❖❖❖

A few days later I asked Dr. Gloom for a pass to go to Gary's hearing.

He frowned. "That's not advisable."

"Why?"

"We don't know what might happen—"

"I know exactly what's going to happen." I launched into an explanation.

"OK," he finally flung over his shoulder on his way out the door. "But I don't like it."

Early the next morning when Gary arrived, the night orderly came charging in after him. "You'll have to come with me, sir."

"Where?" Gary asked in surprise.

The haughty orderly simply repeated the command.

"I'll be back," Gary said. True to his word, he did come back, along with Dr. Gloom and a man who introduced himself as my doctor's supervisor. *Good. I finally get to meet him.*

As soon as the man opened his mouth, I changed my mind. He had a rude, patronizing manner which was ten times worse than Dr. Gloom's, so I promptly dubbed him "Dr. Doom." While he interrogated me, I pasted on a smile and screened out every trace of emotion from my voice. I'd spent enough time on this floor to learn the unwritten rules of the mind games that were played.

"May I see that?" Gary asked when the disagreeable man finished filling out his official form. The doctor wordlessly handed over the paper.

"You circled 'angry,' " Gary said.

"That's right." Dr. Doom spoke with the air of a dictator used to calling the shots. His nickname fit like a rubber glove.

"She isn't angry," Gary said.

"What would you call her?"

Gary studied the choices. "Compliant."

Dr. Doom pacified us by changing that particular answer, but the outcome remained the same. He placed me on house arrest—called a "mental health hold"—for the next seventy-two hours and took away all of my privileges.

"Now I know how a mouse feels living in a barn full of cats," I said when they left. "Except that I can't run and I have no place to hide."

"I have to go or I'll be late," Gary said, his voice full of emotion, the injustice of Dr. Doom's decision bringing tears to his eyes. "I'll be back this afternoon."

Totally helpless to lift a finger on his behalf, I watched my husband walk out the door. Alone. In the midst of a torrent of tears, an invisible noose tightened.

CHAPTER SIXTEEN

Moving On

————◆—◆—◆—◆—◆————

*L*ater that same morning, Dr. Gloom waltzed back into my room, all smiles. "Vickie, I just talked to one of the counselors over at Craig Hospital. You remember Mandy, don't you?"

I nodded.

"She told me about an apartment complex a couple hours north of Denver, up in Greeley, where you could live by yourself. Attendant care is provided—"

"But I already have a place to live," I said, trying not to sound as ticked off as I felt. "And I have attendant care." *What kind of mind games are you playing now?*

Dr. Gloom frowned. "Mandy is coming over on Monday to tell us more about it. I want you to keep an open mind."

I bit my tongue to keep my emotions in check. "OK." *Why can't he level with me and tell me what's going on?*

That afternoon I caught a glimpse of his un-voiced concerns. When therapy ended, Jackie pushed my chair into a small waiting room at the front of the room where I sat until the orderlies came. Most days I didn't have long to wait, but that day proved different. *Come on, guys, hurry it up! This is about as exciting as watching paint dry.* The minutes rolled by.

Suddenly, as if for the first time, I noticed the bright blue binder resting on my lap. The chart always came down with me to therapy. The *forbidden* chart that nurses, doctors and therapists dutifully wrote in each day but would not allow me to read. I snuck a quick peek around the room. Not a soul in sight.

Nervously I flicked the cover back and began to read. Key phrases leaped off the page. "Gary plans to get a job at Burger King. . . ." *That's a blatant lie!* I read on. "Gary admits that he might leave Vickie in the spring." *We both know that he can't work if we live together under the same roof. We've discussed the possibility . . . but I'm sure it won't happen.*

A few pages farther I came to three words, scrawled by Dr. Gloom himself, that made me gasp. "Highly unstable relationship . . ." *That's not true!*

Losing all track of time, I continued flipping pages with the side of my hand until Jackie walked by and caught me in the act of committing knowledge. With a look of outrage, she slammed the binder shut and handed it to one of the orderlies who had just arrived, with strict instructions for him to carry it from now on.

Gary arrived to find me back in bed for the afternoon, feeling extremely sorry for myself.

"How did the hearing go?" I asked.

"Just the way I thought it would. No surprises. But I've got one for you. Which do you want first—the good news or the bad?"

"Good news? Is there such a thing?"

"You'll be out of here within fifteen days."

"What?"

"I stopped at the library. Now that they've put you on a seventy-two hour hold, you're entitled to have a court-appointed attorney meet with you within five days. The case will go to court no later than ten days after that. One way or another, you're getting out of this place."

"That's the best news I've heard since I got here! What's the bad news?"

"You'll be on 'A' status all weekend."

"That means . . . no pass?"

Gary nodded. "And no going outside without a staff member."

I rolled my eyes.

"By the way," Gary said. "I just noticed this today. At the top of the bulletin board by the nurses' station I saw a copy of patients' rights. When you get up later, I'll show it to you."

I stared at him, dumbfounded. "Patients have rights?"

That weekend I sat in the dayroom, bored to the point of tears, when a new resident walked by. Eyes downcast, misery written all over his face, he plopped down on the couch and stared glumly at the floor. I wanted to wheel over and talk to him, but sitting in the hospital's manual recliner I couldn't go anywhere. Finally I spotted a sympathetic nurse and asked her to push me closer. She introduced me to Jeff and went back to her charting.

"Is this your first day here?" I asked.

"Yeah . . . I miss my girlfriend." He lapsed back into silence and floor-gazing.

I didn't pry.

Finally, he looked up. "I'd like to write to her, but I don't have any paper. Or envelopes. Or stamps." His voice trailed off.

"You can get that from the staff," I said. "There's a list of patients' rights up there on the wall. You're entitled to have writing materials."

Just then my nurse walked by.

"Toni," I called, "I'd like some paper to write a letter—and so would my friend."

She soon returned with a yellow legal tablet, tore half the sheets off for Jeff and handed us each a pen.

"Thanks, Toni."

After she left, Jeff actually cracked a smile.

"Happy writing."

"Thanks." He stood up and headed over to a table.

The rest of the long, dull weekend finally ended without a single trip outside—none of the staff had time. Monday came and went uneventfully.

On Tuesday I asked Dr. Gloom what happened to Mandy.

"Oh, I told her not to come because I knew you weren't interested." *Perceptive man.*

Later that morning a nurse told me that my attorney would be in shortly. *Now we're getting somewhere!* Soon, a stranger in a three-piece suit walked through the door. I took an instant dislike to him.

"Hello, I'm Jack," he said, speaking very slowly.

"Hello, Jack," I said, mimicking his patronizing tone. "Do you have a last name, Jack?"

"Cunningham."

I plunged in. "Well, Jack Cunningham, I understand that in order for me to get out of this place, I'll have to go to court."

"Oh, don't worry. These things never go that far," he said with a wave of his hand. "Your doctor will release you before it comes down to that. Here's my card." I cradled it in the palm of my hand. When I looked up, he'd disappeared. *Great. I get an attorney who plans to do absolutely nothing on my behalf.*

"Come on in, Matt," I said when I saw my friend at the door. "What's up?"

"My doctor wants me to go to some drug and alcohol treatment place where I'd be locked up for ninety days. I don't want to give up beer and pot—there's nothing to replace it with." Matt scowled. "I also went to the dental clinic downstairs. My teeth are so bad, they want to pull all of them and give me false teeth. I don't want that, either, so after lunch I'm leaving."

"You're breaking out?"

"It won't be hard. They don't watch the door all the time." He picked up his guitar and began to strum, but stopped when someone entered the room.

I turned my head and did a double take. "Mary! Matt, this is one of the counselors Gary and I used to see."

After introductions, Matt left us alone.

"What are you doing here?"

"Your doctor asked me if I would come to see you. He wants me to continue meeting with you after you leave. How are you doing?"

"Pretty good," I said. "I couldn't have said this last month—and I can't explain it—but I'm actually glad to be alive. . . ."

By the time Mary left, I felt ready to march back into battle against the god-docs and the court-appointed attorney. That evening Gary and I talked over our situation.

"Short of hiring our own attorney, which we can't afford to do, we're stuck with this guy," Gary said.

"I hope he's right about them letting me out. I can't set up an appointment at Craig to try out power chairs until I know when I'm getting out of here."

"I'll check out the cost of renting a power recliner," Gary said.

"Good. I don't want to go back to using my manual chair. I still get dizzy sitting up. It was only last week that I could sit up high enough in bed—without passing out—to feed myself break-fast. Then, half the staff accused me of being lazy because I wasn't feeding myself six weeks ago!"

The following week, Dr. Gloom stopped me in the dayroom after lunch. "We're going to have a treatment planning meeting later today. Your nurse will bring you in."

"What time?" I asked.

"It will start at 1:00."

I looked at my watch. "But that's in ten minutes! I don't have enough time to call Gary and ask him to come. Why didn't you tell me sooner?"

Dr. Gloom looked away. "I just found out."

As Toni wheeled me into the conference room, silence, frowns and tension met me at the door and escorted me to a large, oblong table. There they sat—nurses, aides, god-docs and social workers. I counted them. *Eight wolves against one gimpy lamb. God, where are You? Why do I have to go through this by myself? They're going to eat me alive!* When I saw Dr. Doom, my heart beat so fast it threatened to leap out of my chest. *Calm down, Vickie. Just play the game. Do not show emotion. Do not get angry. Your freedom depends on it.*

"Vickie," Dr. Doom began, "I still don't see that anything has changed at home. . . ."

Once again I voiced my plans to get a power wheelchair and go back to school. The questions dragged on.

"And what if you can't make enough money to pay your expenses once the PASS plan runs out?"

"What if the world ends tomorrow?" I quipped. No one smiled or spoke until Dr. Doom continued grilling me. At last, the meeting ended.

Exhausted, I slept well that night. Early the next morning I awoke with a feeling of anticipation. The attorney would meet with Gary and me and finally prepare to represent me next week.

That morning I had a meeting with Dr. Gloom. A few hours later, Gary motored through the door in a power wheelchair.

"You got it! I can't wait to try it out! Perfect timing too."

"What do you mean?"

"Dr. Gloom finally popped the question. The lawyer was right all along."

"He's letting you out?"

"Yeah. Tomorrow."

Gary moved the hospital's manual chair out of the way, transferred my cushion over and set me down in the new motorized model.

"Look out, world. Here I come." I checked out the power switch and nudged the round ball on the control box with my right hand. The chair shot forward. Quickly pulling my hand away, I almost fell out when it jerked to a sudden halt.

"Looks like this might take some practice," Gary said. "It's a good thing this place has wide hallways."

Nudge by nudge, I lurched out of the room.

Zac saw me coming. "You're driving!"

I grinned. "Scary, huh."

The next day Gary and I met with Dr. Gloom and signed an official list of dos and don'ts, promising, among other things, that we would both continue to see Mary and that I would call someone on the floor if I felt suicidal. When the meeting ended, Gary and I turned and looked at each other.

"I'm free!"

Gary gave me a hug. "Let's pack before—"

"He changes his mind," I chimed in. We both laughed.

"See, great minds do think alike."

Out in the dayroom I spotted a familiar figure talking to one of the nurses. *Uh oh.* When the nurse left, I motored closer. "Matt, what are you doing here? Did you get caught?"

"No, I just stopped in to say good-bye. I'm heading down to Texas." *Huh? How can he get away with this? He takes off, waltzes back in and no one even raises an eyebrow?* Just then Dr. Gloom approached so I kept my questions to myself.

"Good luck, Matt," I said. "I'm leaving too. If you ever get back to Denver, Gary and I are in the phone book. Look us up. We only live about twenty minutes away."

Gary made numerous trips to the van with loads of stuff, but at last my turn came. We both said good-bye to the aides and nurses on the floor. Rolling through the double doors for the last time, excitement mingled with fear and doubt. *Did my forbidden chart speak the truth? Will Gary really wind up moving out?*

CHAPTER SEVENTEEN

New
Beginnings

◆━◆━◆━◆━◆

*L*ong after I heard Gary's deep, rhythmic breathing, the deafening silence kept me awake. I marveled at the quiet darkness, the intimacy of lying with my husband, the lack of strangers parading through the room at will. The comfort of home filled my whole being.

When daylight washed the world anew, I opened my eyes in wonder, half-expecting to find myself back on the psych ward.

"Are you awake?" Gary asked.

I turned my head. "Yeah. Just checking to make sure this isn't a dream."

He moved closer. "It's not."

Surely we'll come up with a way to stay together. Won't we? I pushed my worries aside and slammed the door on them. No way would I let them spoil this special moment. Somehow, somewhere we'd find an answer. Government red tape couldn't tangle our lives forever, could it?

Please, God. Please give Gary something worthwhile to do with his time that will make him happy. Please don't let him start drinking again.

With no attendant care coming in until Monday morning, we enjoyed the luxury of sleeping late. On Saturday afternoon, a stray thought popped into my mind. Weeks earlier one of my nurses had described her church in glowing terms. At the time attending had sounded like a good idea, but I knew Gary wouldn't want to take me. And what was the point? God had come to my rescue in the hospital, so He was already a part of my life, wasn't He? With the matter settled as far as I was concerned, I enjoyed sleeping in on Sunday too.

"Why did I decide to continue with physical therapy?" I asked Gary Tuesday morning.

"I believe it was part of the agreement you signed to get released," he stated matter-of-factly.

"Oh, yeah."

When we pulled into the hospital parking lot, a feeling of dread washed over me. After therapy, I turned to Gary. "I'd like to go upstairs and say 'hi' to Jeff and whoever else is still around."

"Sure you can handle that?"

I grinned. "As long as you don't leave my side at any time."

When we cruised onto the ward, Sherri, the psychologist, immediately darted over. "Have you heard about Matt?"

"Matt? Yeah, I saw him before I left Friday. He told me he was going back to Texas."

"Will you step outside in the hall for a minute?"

By now, Dr. Gloom and the head nurse had also zeroed in on us. Looking equally distressed, they wordlessly followed us out. By the time Sherri steered us to a quiet corner just past the elevators, I had a bad feeling about this little impromptu meeting. No one said a word for the longest time, so I finally spoke.

"He killed himself, didn't he?"

"Yes," Sherri answered softly. "He came back into the facility and told us he was going down to the ER for a minute. That's where it happened. . . ." The bearers of bad tidings continued to stare, as if they expected me to lose control and need an escort back to my old room.

I looked into each of their faces but could not bring myself to voice my somber thoughts. *We all failed him.* Instead, I turned to Gary. "I want to leave now." In silence, Gary and I headed toward the elevator.

On the way home after PT, my guilt launched an attack. "I feel so bad. Could we have helped him? Could we have done something?"

"I don't think so," Gary said. "He needed someone who could have helped him get his head on straight—"

"And given him some encouragement," I added. "Which is precisely why I want to go back to school. When we get home, I'm calling the university to find out how to apply."

In the days ahead, Gary and I gradually drifted back into our own separate worlds. Communication did not improve.

Two weeks later Gary drove me to Craig for my yearly reevaluation. Between tests, I tried out different chairs. Once I made the decision, only a two-month wait separated me from my new custom-built power recliner.

* * *

"Hmmm. This doesn't look very good," Gary said one night a few weeks later. "It's open."

"What's open?" I asked.

"That spot on your pelvic bone we've been watching."

"Let me see." Gary positioned me on my side and held up the mirror. Since it looked insignificant to me, my doctor's advice came as a shock: Stay in bed for ten days.

While I grudgingly did my "down time," I had to skip my weekly counseling sessions with Mary, so Gary went without me. Because my government benefits still prevented him from working, Mary tried once again to persuade him to try volunteer work. This time he agreed and two afternoons the following week he began tutoring math for a class of adolescents at a nearby mental health center. Eight days into the mandatory bed rest I quit complaining about the pressure sore, stopped worrying about the school application and concentrated on breathing.

Back at Craig's clinic, Dr. Wicks took a chest x-ray, prescribed wonder drugs (antibiotics) and handed me some medication to use with my breathing machine. Gary gave me treatments every four hours during the day, but three weeks later, I needed them around the clock.

Every day I pushed down my growing sense of insecurity. *What if Gary finally decides he's had enough—that it's time to "get a life"?*

In January, on Dr. Wicks' advice, I signed myself into Swedish Hospital. In my abundant free time between breathing treatments, I tried to analyze what had changed since last winter when I didn't consider life worth living. *This doesn't make any sense. I should be depressed that I'm back in a hospital . . . with pneumonia . . . but I'm not. How come? God, is this Your doing? Maybe You're more real than I thought.*

One afternoon, during my brief time up in the chair, I went exploring. Out in one of the lounges I came across two other patients in power chairs. Motoring closer, I introduced myself.

"I'm John and this is Eldon," said a sandy-haired man about my age.

"What kind of chair is that?" Eldon asked.

"Everest and Jennings," I said. "I just got it a couple of weeks ago. What kind is yours?" Half an hour of conversation later, the respiratory therapist tracked me down and I went back to bed.

Ten days later, Medicaid regulations pronounced me healthy, took out my IV and sent me home with oral antibiotics. Gary continued giving me breathing treatments and our conversations revolved around my health. Two-and-a-half weeks later, still hacking, I returned to Swedish. This time my lungs felt like a glue factory. From my hospital bed, I watched the last half of that bleak February turn into March. When I finally left, I knew every respiratory therapist in the place.

At last able to draw a deep breath without coughing, I sat at the computer and pored over college application essay questions: Why did I want to go into social work? What life experiences contributed to this desire?

I had a good friend named Matt. . . .

Six double-spaced pages later I sent off my answers and Gary took me over to the campus for a tour.

"It looks practically deserted," I said. Half a dozen cars lined the parking lot and only a handful of students scurried about. We turned off University Boulevard and pulled into a handicap spot.

"Maybe it's spring break," Gary said.

"That would be nice. I'm not ready to face a bunch of strangers."

We headed toward a double-wide sidewalk, but suddenly the building directly in front of me caught my eye and I lurched to a halt. No matter which way I turned, the buildings all looked the same. Mirror images slammed home a message as sharp as barbed wire.

Four years ago, I had barely noticed them, but that day they seemed to spring up everywhere and block my every move. What, gangs and guns? No, something far more common. Steps! Cold, indifferent slabs of concrete. Steps and stares. *Welcome to the real world, Vickie.*

"They must have built this place before the invention of wheelchairs," I muttered. "I thought you said it was accessible."

"The woman I talked to told me you'd have no problem getting into the social work building."

"Maybe she didn't understand—"

Just then we rounded a corner and saw it. The red brick structure was the same except for a gentle slope that blazed a smooth trail to the front door.

I had no problem motoring to the top, but saw no square handicap button for me to push to trigger an automatic door. "Not very user-friendly. Will you do the honors?"

Gary pulled one of the heavy glass doors open and I rolled inside. When the door swung shut, a hush descended. We saw no students, heard no buzz of voices. At the back of the room a woman sat at a lone desk. We approached her. I hid behind Gary and let him do the talking.

"Excuse me, my wife is thinking about going to school here. Is it OK if we look around?"

"Sure. It's pretty quiet today. Most of the students have already left for spring break."

She didn't even gawk at me.

"Do you want to check out the elevator?" Gary asked.

"Yeah." I motored the short distance to the shiny silver doors, pulled up parallel and easily tapped the low black button with the side of my handbrace.

The doors instantly sprang open. I wheeled inside and Gary stepped in beside me. A few seconds passed before the doors closed. "That's a relief," I said. "At least I won't get crunched getting in. Now to see if I can make it go anywhere."

Again I found I could easily reach the low panel and punched "B." Our metal chariot smoothly delivered us to the basement. We went exploring and found two deserted classrooms. When I wheeled through the extra-wide doorways, I found that I had ample room to maneuver.

The third room we entered had some old, well-used couches scattered around, a couple of soda machines, a sink, some tables and chairs: the lounge. Overall, it appeared a comfortable place to hang out.

While I motored through vacant classrooms, I began to consider the reality of what lay ahead. What if I couldn't remember how to study? Sure, maybe I could make the elevator go up and down, but what if I couldn't hack the academic part?

After I rolled through every doorway, Gary held the front door open and I motored back out into the bright sunlight.

"What do you think?" he asked.

"Gee, I don't know if it will work."

"Why not? You can get around—"

"Sure, I can manage the elevator and get into all the classrooms."

"And once you're inside, you don't have to leave the building all day so you won't need help with your coat."

"Yes, but. . . ." My voice trailed off.

"But what?" Gary probed.

"Well, I can bring a sack lunch . . . but what if I need someone to refill my cup at lunch?" I blurted.

"Stop and think about it," Gary said. "What kind of people go into social work?"

"Well, people that want to help other people." The light finally dawned. "So maybe someone wouldn't mind giving me water!" We looked at each other and burst out laughing. As we headed home, I thought *Maybe I* can *do this.*

◆━◆━◆━◆━◆

Three weeks later, I received good news. The University of Denver had accepted me into their social work program. Upon learning that my plans would crystalize into reality come fall, Gary made plans of his own.

"I told Mary I'd give volunteer work a fair try," he said one evening, "but it's not enough. . . ."

My stomach churned. "It's not?"

"No." He spoke so softly that I had to strain to catch his words. "I feel like a bum because I'm not making money. I need to get a real job . . . I have to move out. . . ." Gary avoided my gaze. "We've discussed this before."

A sigh escaped my lips. "I know. I thought by now something would have changed. The laws about you earning money . . . my need for government benefits . . . the paralysis . . . something! But this is the same problem we faced when we moved in here."

Gary stood up and began to pace. Glumly, he stared off into the distance, started to speak, then stopped, as if struggling for the right words. "I— I've been looking into apartments downtown."

"Apartments?" *He can't be serious. There's got to be a better solution than this!*

In a wooden monotone, he continued. "I found one that I can afford and I gave the manager a deposit."

"A deposit?" The words sliced into my heart like a scalpel. I looked into his eyes.

He returned my gaze, his face a mixture of sadness and resignation. "I have a plane reservation for two weeks from today to go back and visit my father. When I return, I'll move into the apartment."

Stunned, I could not speak. No words formed on my lips. No rational thoughts broke through the dense fog that filled my head.

"You can do this, Vickie. You've come a long way since the accident. You've already proved that you can live here by yourself."

"Well, yeah. That doesn't scare me anymore...."

"And you have morning attendant care in place, so it will only take a phone call to let the agency know that you need someone for evenings.... You have some great neighbors you can call on in a pinch.... For that matter, once I'm back, you can call me too."

I wiped my tears away with the back of one hand and managed a smile.

After Gary situated me in bed that night, he spent the rest of the evening out in the living room with Beethoven's Ninth and beer.

God? Can You heal a broken heart?

◆◆◆◆◆◆◆◆

The crisp spring morning dawned bright and clear. I had evening attendant care all lined up. I had friends, neighbors and relatives programmed into my telephone. I knew that I could live here by myself. But at the moment, none of that mattered.

A final good-bye hug, a last kiss and Gary was gone. The door to our crumbled marriage banged shut when he drove off into the sunrise. *It's over.*

My heart mourned this final deathblow to our marriage. Tears befuddled my thinking. Time ground to a halt. *He's gone—and I start graduate school in the fall.*

Aimlessly I wandered back inside and finally pulled up to the telephone. While staring into the empty bedroom at the far end of the house, I punched in a number. My therapist answered. Without pausing for breath I blurted, "It's the fourth anniversary of my accident and Gary just left."

"Oh, Vickie!" Mary exclaimed. "I'm so sorry. Did this come as a big shock?"

I sighed. "No. I guess I've seen it coming for a long time, but it still hit me like a sledgehammer."

"How do you feel?"

"Lousy. But in an odd way," I said wistfully, "this is probably the kindest thing we could have done for each other. It's a new beginning—for both of us. Now I have to stop depending on Gary for everything. And chances are, he'll stop drinking because my benefits won't prevent him from working. But the pain . . ."

After I hung up, I took a deep breath. *This is it, Little Circus Girl. Like it or not, the show must go on.*

PART FIVE

Soaring Again

CHAPTER EIGHTEEN

On My Own

"Stop that!" Astonished at her audacity, I reached out a clumsy hand while she deliberately strolled across my keyboard—again! A long string of gibberish marched across the screen. Agitated that I would dare raise my voice to her, the nine-week-old troublemaker nimbly jumped to the top of the monitor. Haughty green eyes flashed me an icy stare as if to say, "Oh yeah? What can you do about it, gimp?" She knew I couldn't reach her on her lofty perch.

"You brat! Get down from there!"

Puddin had only arrived a week ago, but she'd already turned my neat, orderly life into chaos. With school starting in less than two weeks, everything had just begun to come together quite nicely.

"Whatever are we going to do, Punkin?" My other cat merely blinked, rolled over and curled up again with one paw over his nose—as if to fend off another ambush by the resident kitty-terrorist.

At last, bored with her human, Puddin jumped down and pranced away. Shaking my head, I turned back to the screen to delete her handiwork from my "homework." To get a jump on the workload, I had purchased the required book for one of my upcoming classes and read a chapter each week for the entire summer. I finished typing in notes for chapter 10, saved them and loaded my "urgent to do" list.

Let's see . . . Vocational Rehabilitation is finally in place to pay for extra attendant care, books and part of the tuition, so I can check that off. Lapboard—finished! I typed in another big "X." *Thank goodness Gary is willing to help me.* Weeks ago I had sketched a design for a lapboard. Then the previous night, Gary had cut a piece of Peg-Board™ into a rectangular shape, turning it into a mobile desk that my aide could attatch to the armrests of my chair.

Thinking back to all the changes my battered heart had weathered since that fateful day the previous spring when he told me his plans, a lone tear squeezed out. *Look on the bright side. Be glad you and Gary are still friends. Be glad he signed up at your agency to work for you as an aide.* Our marriage had begun turning into a nurse/patient relationship long before we split up, but even so, my heart refused to be glad.

Just then the door creaked open and Gary poked his head in the bedroom. "I need to run an errand. Do you want to stay up a little longer?"

I smiled. "Yes.

My chest felt tight—as if a giant weight pinned me down. I felt hot—too hot. In my half-dream, half-awake state of limbo, I gasped for air. My sleep-drugged mind jumped to hasty conclusions— pneumonia! I forced my eyelids apart, but my eyes quickly told a different tale—a furry brown one.

"Punkin! How many times do I have to tell you? You're too heavy to lie on my neck!" The pudgy feline merely purred.

"Don't say I didn't warn you." I blew in his ear. He shook his head but snuggled back down. I blew again. The annoyed creature finally marched away. I had learned long ago that shouting at him merely made my voice hoarse.

Glancing at the clock, I suddenly remembered. *Opening day! Can I really do this?* Even my but- terflies had butterflies.

The sound of Sandy's car pulling into the drive- way assured me that yes, indeed, I *would* do this. The morning routine—bed bath, breakfast, dress- ing, rolling out of the bedroom—passed in a blur and all too soon I found myself in the van. Four miles later, when Sandy turned into the school parking lot, the sight brought me up short.

"The place is swarming with students!"

"Well, it is the first day of school," Sandy replied.

After she unloaded me and tied my lapboard on, Sandy walked me to the social work building. Once inside, I found myself surrounded by friendly faces. I recognized many fellow students from orientation the week before, but few names stuck.

"Need anything?" Sandy asked.

"No, I think I'm set. See you at 3:30." I watched her walk back down the ramp.

"Hi, Vickie."

I turned away from the window to see a young blond-haired man. His wire-rim glasses and brief-case gave him a scholarly look. "Hi! It's good to see you again . . . Phil, right?"

His smile answered my question. "Where are you doing your internship?" he asked.

"Allison Health Care. It's a nursing home. I can't believe we start next week. I don't know anything yet! Where are you . . ." My voice trailed off when I noticed the silence and the absence of other students.

Phil calmly voiced my panicky thoughts. "I guess we better get to class."

Social Work Foundations met in the basement, so I motored toward the elevator. Phil pushed the button and rode down with me. Once the doors opened we parted company and I motored through the first door on the right. A room full of students sat in a circle. My face felt hot when all eyes momentarily turned toward me.

The buzz of pre-class chatter dwindled when the instructor finally walked through the door, closing it behind him. I groaned. He didn't look at all like a Mrs. Parsons.

Slowly I motored forward, mumbled an apology to the teacher and turned around to leave. *Uh oh.* The closed door had a smooth round doorknob—a device totally beyond my grasp. Self-conscious as a teenager sporting a mouthful of braces, I asked for help.

When the door opened, I escaped to the silent, empty hall where I checked my schedule more carefully and headed to the right classroom. I spied Phil sitting front row center, but I cowered in the back.

Soon a teacher arrived—a female teacher. "Welcome to Social Work Foundations," Mrs. Parsons began. "I would like each of you to introduce yourselves and tell us a little about why you're here."

My heart began to pound. *Please, God, don't let my mind go blank.*

My pen hung down from a plastic loop slung around my joystick. To keep my panic in check, I reached out, lifted it up with my handbrace, pushed the pen through the spring opening and flipped open a notebook. When the first student began to speak, I jotted down his name and a brief description. "Steve Allred—grey sweater-vest, short sleeve shirt, brown hair." Already behind, I shortened descriptions and scrawled faster.

"Peggy Blatt, blond, blue blouse."
Better.

Soon all eyes zeroed in on me. *Show time!* I licked my dry lips. "I'm Vickie Baker and I ... ah ... I had an accident a little over four years ago and ... um. ..." A quick glance around revealed a room full of empathetic faces. Encouraged, I continued. "I'm here because I've finally taken my focus off of 'poor me' and now I want to do something to help other people." *Whew.*

When the last student finished speaking, class began. Within minutes a sinking feeling washed over me. My hasty handwriting became messier and messier. Falling farther and farther behind, I finally stopped writing altogether.

Ten minutes later the teacher announced a break and told us about some forms we needed to pick up on a table by the mailboxes upstairs. I made a mental note to have Sandy pick them up for me.

A kind, motherly looking woman to my left, Mary Buck, turned toward me. "I noticed you were having trouble keeping up. Would you like to borrow my notes?"

"Thanks, but I'd never be able to copy all of your notes during the break. But would you mind . . ." The question, poised on my tongue, refused to emerge while my thoughts battled back and forth.

Go on, ask! What are you afraid of? What's the worst thing that could happen?

She might say "no."

Can you live with that?

Yes.

Then ask!

"Uh, Mary? Would you mind if I made a copy of your notes after class?"

A broad smile lit up her face. "That would be no problem at all."

Most of the students stretched, walked around and eventually drifted out the door. I did a much-needed weight shift by reclining into a horizontal position. Soon, someone approached and set some papers on my lapboard.

"I picked up your forms and checked your mailbox."

I sat back up. *Grey sweater-vest* . . . "Steve, right?"

He smiled. "Right."

"Thanks, but you didn't have to go to all that trouble."

"It was no trouble at all. I wanted to pick up my stuff and Baker comes right after Allred. Uh . . . could you have gotten them yourself?"

I grinned. "No. I was hoping I'd remember to ask my aide when she came to pick me up, but I probably would have forgotten. I feel so overwhelmed."

"You too?" Steve asked in surprise. "You mean I'm not the only one?"

When the break ended, Mary slid back into her seat and turned toward me. "It's all set. They'll let me use the copy machine upstairs—the one reserved for the teachers."

"You are a lifesaver!"

When class ended, Mary charged out the door and returned with copies of her exquisite "I used to be a teacher" notes before I'd even turned around to head to the lounge for lunch. By the time 3:30 rolled around, I'd made many new friends and had more reading assignments than I knew what to do with. Gary arrived that night to find me crying and coughing.

"I need a way to read in bed," I wailed.

He frowned. "We've already been through this. If you stick to the schedule we worked out, three hours of study a week for every hour of credit you're taking, you'll do just fine."

Stressed to the max with work already piling up, I quickly rolled into a rut and didn't emerge until the end of the quarter. Weekends found me reading, studying or cranking out papers. I even used my "extra hour"—the one we get when daylight savings time ends—to study for a test!

I never would have considered squandering Sunday mornings on something as frivolous as going to church. Yet even in the midst of all my busyness, it felt like something was missing. But what?

◆◆◆◆◆

During the last week of the quarter, a love/hate relationship suddenly sprang up between my computer and me. By 8 p.m. Sunday night my neck ached and my eyes smarted. I glared at the computer.

Gary arrived to find me muttering incoherent threats. "What's wrong?"

"It finally happened."

"What happened?"

"My anxiety rubbed off on this stupid machine."

"Don't be silly—"

"I knew you'd take sides with the computer," I snapped. "I've been staring at this screen since I got up this morning. I ran the spell check and was all set to print my paper when the hard drive ate it. It ate my term paper! Half of it's gone and I still have two more to finish! What am I gonna do?"

"You're going to go to bed."

"What?"

"You're going to bed, and I will work on retrieving your paper."

Exhausted, I finally agreed.

Gary fiddled with the computer until nearly midnight. "I think it's fixed," he said. "Your entire paper came up on the screen. Call me tomorrow if you have any problems."

"Thanks."

The following day I didn't leave my bedroom until 3:30 in the afternoon. Once Sandy had me up in my chair, I headed straight for the computer. When I punched in my school file, my entire term paper, like a kept promise, appeared on the screen. *If only the promises Gary and I had once made to each other could . . . Stop it, Vickie, it's over. It's been over for a long time. Focus on the term papers.*

I turned on the printer, clicked the "magic" button and held my breath. Page after perfect page of prose printed out. With my handbrace, I held the fanfold paper and watched the stack grow on my lapboard. At last I read the beautiful words, "The End."

By lunchtime, I finished editing paper number two and once again, it successfully printed out. Sandy returned. At my request, she set some coldcuts on my left hand. I nibbled while tapping the keyboard with a pen stuck in the handbrace on my other hand. Soon, hungry cats wandered in and began to circle.

"Sandy," I called, "I need you to get these guys out of here and shut the door. I'm running out of time!"

In my cat-free environment, peace and perspiration prevailed, but moments later Puddin jumped up on the table and headed for the keyboard.

"Don't you dare," I snarled. "Sandy, I thought you closed the door. How did Puddin get back in?"

"Punkin opened it."

"Great. A cat who knows how to pull on levers to open doors and one who accompanies me on the keyboard. Just great."

Sandy quickly retrieved the cat while I contemplated murder.

An hour later, the computer played hide-and-seek with my last paper. Practically in tears, I called Gary. Over the speakerphone he talked me through the problem. Finally my last paper rolled off the printer. I tore it off, Sandy jumped in her car to drive it over to campus and I dissolved into a puddle of tears.

The next day I called my classmate, Peggy, to see how she had fared.

"I still have two papers to finish," she confided, "but with six weeks off I can take my time."

"Six weeks? How can that be?"

"I got an extension until the first day of winter quarter." I almost fell out of my chair. *An extension? Man, do I ever have a lot to learn!*

CHAPTER NINETEEN

Soaring to New Heights

◆━◆━◆━◆━◆

*M*y attention wandered away from the textbook and riveted on the clock. Eight minutes till curfew—*if* she arrived on time. I had another new aide—a friend of Sandy's who had signed up at my agency. I huffed one of my brave-martyr sighs at the cat curled up on the bed, but Punkin paid no heed. He'd heard it all before.

For the most part, I liked living by myself, but I didn't like the hassle of training new aides. And some aides I just didn't get along with.

Please, God, let this one have some common sense. And let her have . . .

Bam. Bam. Bam.

I gulped. *Please let her have intelligence.*

Backing out of the bedroom, I reluctantly wheeled to the front door to let her in. *Showtime,*

Vickie! When the young woman stepped inside, I did a double take.

She grinned. "Not what you were expecting, am I?"

"Well, ah . . . no," I stammered while my face turned various shades of red. With a name like Mae-Lynne, I had pictured a soft-spoken, dainty slip of a girl, her black hair tied back with a pink ribbon. The attractive woman with beautiful, curly red hair who had insistently pounded on my door did not fit the picture.

Mae-Lynne followed me into the living room. "You live here by yourself?"

"Yeah. My husband and I separated a year ago last spring. This past summer we got a . . . er . . . we made it permanent." I couldn't bring myself to say the ugly word and thanks to my grueling summer school schedule, the finality of the divorce had not sunk in yet.

"Where would you like me to start?" Mae-Lynne asked.

"With my lapboard. I need you to unstrap it and set it on the table.

"What's next?"

"Follow me," I said, blazing a path over the linoleum and through the shag to my bedroom. "I need you to pull the covers back." In short order, I pulled up next to the bed. After Mae-Lynne put my nightshirt on, I added, "My pants velcro down both sides. They're really easy to take off once I'm in bed."

She gave me a funny look. "Why don't I unvelcro them now and leave them on the chair when I transfer you?"

Amazed, I stared at her. "Why? Because I never thought of it before, that's why!"

We both burst out laughing.

"I like your initiative," I said.

"The Lord helps me in so many ways throughout the day," Mae-Lynne began. "I don't know what I'd do without Him."

Uh oh. Sandy warned me that she's into religion.

"I can't stand it when someone tries to save me!" I said. "I remember a date I had fifteen years ago in college. This guy arrived at my dorm room with a Bible in his hand! I guess he was planning on spending a quiet evening reading to me or something."

Mae-Lynne laughed. "He was an eager beaver."

I scowled. "He asked me if I was saved. I had no idea what that meant, but I sure didn't want religion crammed down my throat. That was our first—and last—date."

"Jesus didn't cram religion down anyone's throat," Mae-Lynne said. "He just loved them. He met them right where they were."

"Do you think He would have gone skydiving with me?"

"You used to skydive?" Her eyes grew big and she gave a low whistle. "I'm sure He was with you when you went. I was going to do that once. Before we were married, my husband and I had the money all saved up. But the Lord had other plans. We had three kids and the money went for other things. We never did get around to making that jump."

"Have you heard of tandem skydiving?" I asked.

Mae-Lynne shook her head.

"The FAA approved it about about five years ago," I said, delighted to change the topic. "The back of the student's harness attaches to hardware on the front of the instructor's harness. Both the student and the instructor face the same direction and leave the plane together. The instructor can pull the ripcord to deploy the chute, steer the canopy and land without help from the student. That makes it possible for me to skydive again.

"In fact," I added, "how about when I make a jump, you make one too?"

"You're on."

"Great!" I exclaimed. "Two weeks from Saturday I'm making a tandem skydive." Seeing her incredulous expression, I grinned. "Not what you were expecting, am I?"

I awakened at dawn, nearly beside myself with excitement. *Today's the day!* While I waited for Mae-Lynne to arrive, my mind drifted back to the various events leading up to this day. The planning for the jump began when an old skydiving buddy, Stan McGrew, materialized on my doorstep during a short layover. While we reminisced about old times at Littleton Airport, the topic of tandem skydiving came up.

Two weeks later I got a call. "It's all set," Stan said. "I talked to the folks out at the Loveland/Ft. Collins airport. They're quite willing to work with you. Here's the number. . . ."

Just then Mae-Lynne walked through the front door, jolting me back to the here and now. I flashed her a smile.

"Ready for this?" she asked.

"You bet! Let's get this show on the road."

An hour later Mae-Lynne loaded me into the van. I rambled nonstop all the way out to the airport—my first time at a drop zone since before the accident. When the lift lowered my chair from the van, I felt self-conscious. From nearby, jumpers curiously eyed my cumbersome electric wheelchair. The somber thoughts evident on their faces echoed through the deafening silence: "There but for the grace of God . . ."

Suddenly, a friendly face swam into focus. "Hi. I'm Rick. Are you Vickie?"

I looked up. "How did you know? Wait, let me guess . . . the wheelchair gave me away, right?"

Rick smiled.

Another jumper approached. "Hi, Vickie, do you remember me? John Gordon. Everyone calls me Big John."

"Yes!" I exclaimed. "You used to jump out at Longmont, didn't you?"

Soon a few other jumpers wandered over and introduced themselves. We began swapping skydiving stories and I felt right at home.

My instructor, Rick, explained the procedure for making the jump and two skydivers helped wrestle my body into a jumpsuit and harness. After Rick climbed aboard, Big John carried me over to the Cessna 206 and set me inside.

At 10,500 feet above the ground Rick opened the door. My heartbeat quickened. *No problem with my low blood pressure now.* He moved us closer to the door and let our legs dangle out. The sight almost took my breath away: sunshine, clear skies, lots of altitude—jump run! What a delicious yet almost forgotten feeling. After all, quadriplegics aren't supposed to go leaping out of airplanes, are they?

Rick leaned forward to spot. "Five left!"

The pilot corrected.

"Five more left . . . Cut!"

The pilot reduced the speed, Rick leaned forward and we were out. Falling free. Free falling. Memories flooded over me as the wind rushed past. Plummeting toward earth, we built up speed. I had forgotten how difficult breathing can become when you're hurtling through the air at 120 miles an hour.

At 4,500 feet, when the tiny specks on the ground began to resemble human beings, Rick pulled the ripcord.

Pow!

The parachute slammed open and I reeled from the abrupt jolt. Funny, I hadn't remembered opening shock as such a bone-wrenching experience. It felt like all my teeth jarred loose!

A euphoric feeling washed over me as we floated gently down. Transported back in time, the silent "hush" I remembered so well from past jumps made my heart soar. My gaze traveled from the serene farmland far below to the colorful canopy above my head. For those few brief moments in time, suspended halfway between heaven and earth, the paralysis didn't matter.

The parachute danced in the sparkling blue sky as all too soon we made one last turn to set up an approach pattern. A light breeze made for a perfect stand-up landing. When Rick touched down, two jumpers reached out to steady us and someone else wheeled my chair over.

"What do you think?" Rick asked. "Was it just like you remembered?"

"Yes! What a rush! I want to do this again!"

The whole way home I couldn't stop grinning.

Lying in bed that night, I tapped a few buttons on my speakerphone and a preprogrammed number efficiently dialed itself.

"Hello," a familiar voice chimed. "How was your day?"

"Well, now that it's after the fact, I guess I can tell you—"

"You jumped out of an airplane!" This woman had me pegged—she handled my antics awfully well for a mom. A month earlier I had told her about tandem skydiving and asked if she wanted to know ahead of time should I ever try it. She briefly considered before saying, "No." Being the conscientious daughter that I am, I honored her request.

"Tell me all about it!" Mom's voice broke into my thoughts.

I explained the facts, but I couldn't recapture the elusive feeling. The risk-taking "high" that I'd worshiped my whole life had vanished into thin air the moment Rick's feet hit the ground.

✦✦✦✦✦

Mae-Lynne, a more "down-to-earth" sort than I, copped out that day. "I didn't think you'd actually go through with it," she said. "I would have made a jump, but I couldn't afford it. Honest!"

"Yeah, right. I know a chicken when I see one."

Over the following weeks we became good friends and she proved to be an excellent aide. I liked her easygoing manner, even if she did sprinkle conversations with "the Lord this," and "the Lord that." From her sincere tone of voice and from the sense of calm which emanated from her, she made it sound like she knew God personally.

But unlike my college date, Mae-Lynne didn't try to push anything on me. In fact, she remained perfectly content to keep this mystery to herself—which drove me nuts! What did she know that I didn't know? She seemed to have a handle on the joy that I only experienced when leaping out of airplanes or rappeling off cliffs. I looked forward to the nights when she came.

"I'm thinking about changing churches," she said one night.

"Why?" I asked.

"I want to find one closer to home. My kids don't like the long drive. This Sunday will probably be our last trip out there."

I didn't say anything, but my conscience nagged me the rest of the visit. Finally, when Mae-Lynne put on her coat to leave, I spoke. "Would you mind if I tagged along? We'd need to take my van . . . and you'd have to drive."

A big smile lit up her face. "That would be great."

At 9:15 Sunday morning Mae-Lynne pulled up with her three daughters in tow. She loaded me into my van, her kids jumped in and we took off.

"I agree with your kids," I commented when we pulled into the parking lot. "That *was* a long drive."

When the service let out, we piled back into the van for the long trek back home. Mae-Lynne turned to me. "Besides the fact that it's so far away, what did you think?"

"Well, I liked the music," I said. "But I wasn't crazy about the sermon. It just didn't seem to fit what I'm looking for."

A few weeks later Mae-Lynne and I began "church hopping." We tried a couple of different churches, each with a different atmosphere, but nothing seemed to "click."

One church used what I quickly dubbed the "pity-pat" method. When it was time to greet one another, many smiling faces and eager feet headed my way to give me a big "oh you poor brave thing" hug and a sympathetic pat on my shoulder.

The second church was huge, fancy and impersonal. Mae-Lynne and I felt like two stowaways from the island of misfit toys amidst an ocean of unfamiliar people. When we got to the van after the service, I spoke first. "I'm not exactly sure of what I'm looking for, but I don't think that was it. I need something more personal and a little less intimidating."

Before I knew it, September had arrived and Mae-Lynne and I still hadn't found a church we liked. Then one day I remembered the flier that I had received a couple of months earlier about a new church service. I dug it out, and we saw that it was wheelchair accessible, so we decided to give it a try.

When I motored inside the gymnasium where the service was being held, I saw forty or fifty folding chairs arranged in neat rows. A small group of people—all dressed casually—milled around. Faces turned in our direction when I rolled through the door, but I didn't detect any "pity stares."

A man wearing a brown suit and a broad smile hurried over. "Hello. I'm Pastor Sorensen." He handed us each a bulletin and asked our names.

Two young men wearing dress shirts tucked into their jeans stood off in a corner tuning their guitars. When they finished, they headed over to welcome us. No "pity-pat party" in this place.

Why is everyone being so nice to me? They don't know me from Adam! I've never been to a church like this.

We made our way over to the last row of chairs. Mae-Lynne sat down and I pulled up next to her. The pastor stood up, introduced himself to everyone and explained that they had designed this new service especially for young people. The guitar players began strumming and the small congregation raised their voices in song. I liked the lively, upbeat rhythms of the unfamiliar pieces. When the last, sweet note faded away, the pastor walked to the podium carrying a small Bible.

"I'd like to talk to you about the importance of reading the Bible," he began.

Startled, I jerked my head up. *How does he know I've never read the Bible? Does anyone else know?* I snuck a quick peek around, but no one seemed to pay any attention to me and my silly fears.

The pastor's words reached down into my very soul. "First, we read the Bible to get to know God."

I can learn more about God this way? How come I never knew this?

"Who can give me another reason why it's important to read the Bible?"

One of the guitar players raised his hand.

"Yes, Doug."

"So we know how to live our lives."

God tells us how to live our lives?

"That's right. Now please turn to chapter 9 of Acts, starting with verse 1."

Mae-Lynne reached for a Bible sitting on a vacant chair in front of her, flipped to the right spot and held it where we could both see it.

"You will see that God had a purpose for Saul's life just as He has a purpose for your life."

God has a purpose for my life? Did He have anything to do with keeping me alive when I tried so hard to die? Or when my heart stopped in the hospital?

On that quiet September morning, I learned about Saul's journey on the road to Damascus. Doing fine one minute, Saul was struck totally blind a fraction of a second later. Talk about life-changing! *My journey's been pretty life-changing too.*

When the service ended and we headed out to the parking lot, Mae-Lynne turned to me. "I like this church. How about you?"

"Yes. I didn't know God has a purpose for our lives!"

"Sometimes He has to get our attention first, the way He did with Saul, before we're willing to listen, though."

"You know, I thought life wasn't worth living without an adrenaline rush. I never expected to find it at church!"

Mae-Lynne smiled. "That's the Lord."

"He's real, isn't He? I want to know more about Him."

"Read the Bible, Vickie. Maybe this church has a good Bible study group."

Mae-Lynne put the key in the ignition. An indescribable joy filled my heart and my spirit began to soar.

CHAPTER TWENTY

A New Ringmaster

❖━◆━◆━◆━◆━❖

"Hi, Dad," I said when my father picked up the phone. "How's everything going today?"

"Oh, I can't complain. Your mama stocked the freezer with a week's worth of dinners before she left, so I'm in good shape."

After some small talk about meals, I broached a topic that had become very dear to me. "Dad, this Bible study I'm doing with Pastor Keith is exciting. I never opened a Bible before. What an incredible book!"

"I tried reading the Bible once," my father confided.

"You did?"

"Yeah. But I got hung up in all the begats."

"Start in the New Testament," I urged. "We started in the Gospel of John. Christ's message is really starting to come alive!

"You know," I added, "when Mom gets back, I'm going to ask her why she doesn't read the Bible."

"Now, honey, don't go rocking the boat—"

"I'm just going to ask, Dad. Having a personal relationship with Jesus Christ is the most important thing there is."

"I frequently talk with the 'Man Upstairs,' " my father volunteered.

"You do?" Eager, never-before-voiced questions sprang to mind. I couldn't wait to find out more—and to share with him what I was learning. Mom had told me that growing up Dad went to Sunday school, but his parents never attended church. *What did he learn as a youngster? When did he stop going? And why?* Yet before I could open my mouth, our surprisingly candid conversation abruptly ended.

"Thanks for calling, honey. I'll be talking to you again."

"But Dad—"

"Bye, now."

Click.

Darn. Oh well, we have plenty of time to talk about this again.

A couple of days later Pastor Keith called to let me know he'd be a few minutes late for Bible study and asked if I needed anything. Joking, I said, "Yeah—a banana split."

When I opened the door that afternoon, I gasped. Grinning like a schoolboy with a frog up his sleeve, Pastor Keith stood there holding the biggest banana split I had ever seen.

That day I learned the truth about salvation and eternal life.

We opened to chapter 3 of the study book. "Read the verse at the top—John 3:16," Pastor Keith said.

"For God so loved the world that he gave his one and only Son, that whoever believes in him shall not perish but have eternal life."

"What is God's promise?"

I studied the verse. "That we will have eternal life."

"If? . . ." Pastor Keith prompted.

"If we believe in Him," I said slowly.

"That's right. It's not what we *do*, but what we *believe*. When we acknowledge that Jesus Christ died for our sins and confess our faith in Him, then our sins are forgiven and we're assured of eternal life."

"So we don't have to earn our way into heaven?"

Pastor Keith shook his head and smiled. "God's plan of salvation is awesome, isn't it?"

I nodded.

"I need to ask you something," he continued. "You told me about your experience in the psych ward when you asked God for help, but have you ever asked Jesus to come into your heart?"

I smiled. "Yes. When I read this week's chapter I realized that when I was in the hospital, God made a committment to me and that I needed to make one to Him."

When Pastor Keith read the question, "What gives you assurance that Jesus is your Savior?" I didn't hesitate. "I have confessed my sins and accepted Him—and I believe."

◆◆◆◆◆

An icy December wind canceled out the sun's weak rays while I huddled around the graveside with family and friends. My cheeks felt as numb as my emotions. The week before I'd received a shocking phone call. Mom's tearful words had stunned me. "Honey, your father suffered a heart attack. He . . . he's dead. . . ."

Moments earlier at the service, Mom's priest had used the words quiet, gentle and private to describe my father. Something about this picture grated on my consciousness, but it was nothing I could put a gimpy finger on, so I filed it away to ponder later.

When the incredibly long day finally ended, my thoughts tumbled back to the priest's eulogy.

Quiet. Indeed, even in failing health, my eighty-four-year-old father left this world as quietly as the way he had lived.

Gentle. This captured his peacemaking spirit. It had annoyed me that "don't ruffle feathers or cause waves" had become his way of life.

Private. My father had kept most of his thoughts and emotions to himself up to the very end. Why did that bother me so much?

In the days leading up to Christmas, the truth finally dawned. That one "enlightening" conversation I'd shared with him last fall suddenly took on monumental proportions.

Why didn't I follow through? Why didn't I ask him more about his faith? Why didn't I share God's incredible plan of salvation? Why, God, why?

Talking about God had seemed such a taboo topic and now I would never know more than the fact that my father "frequently talked to the Man Upstairs." My tears flowed freely.

<hr />

That year, my mother and I spent the holidays together doing more mourning than celebrating—until Christmas Eve. After the service at my mother's church that afternoon, we made up a plate of cookies and Mom loaded me into my van. My church's congregation met at one member's house for a time of visiting, friendship and sharing of food before the service. When we pulled into the driveway, twenty or thirty people streamed out of Doug and Lona's house to welcome us and help commandeer my chair up the steps.

Pastor Keith, the first one out the door, gave my mother a big hug. "I'm happy you could join us, Dee. I'm so sorry to hear about your husband."

"Thank you," my mother said, returning his hug. Tears glistened in her eyes, but the warm reception we both received dried her tears and filled my heart with joy.

After about an hour, we all bundled up for the short walk to the church. Pastor Keith handed out candles.

"None for me," I said. "I'm a fire hazard."

"Would you like me to carry yours?" Mom asked, zipping up my jacket.

"Yes. That would be nice."

At the bottom of the steps, side by side, we fell in line with the rest of the small procession. All down the street, candles flickered in warm mittened hands. Frosty breath hung in the frigid night air. A stiff breeze blew, all but drowning out our voices as we sang "Joy to the World." When we reached the church, I heard the jangle of keys before the door flew open and we all hurried inside.

Mae-Lynne helped my mother get my coat off.

"Come sit in the front," Pastor Keith urged everyone.

"Let's start with 'Silent Night.' " he began. "Will everyone please stand?"

I smiled. *On the inside I'm standing.*

When I heard the words "calm and bright" I marveled. Sitting there surrounded by a handful of caring believers, I realized that my life had become calm and bright in a way I'd never dreamed possible. *All because Jesus came to earth and went to the cross—for me. For me!*

The song ended, but the words remained etched in my mind. Pastor Keith began to speak. The story of Christ's birth, which I'd heard my whole life, suddenly came alive.

"Imagine a young teenage couple, far from home," Pastor Keith began. "All of a sudden, the young bride, who is very pregnant, goes into labor.

"How do you think they felt when innkeeper after innkeeper turned them away and they were forced to take refuge in a smelly barn? Scared? Homesick? Awestruck with the role they were to play in God's great plan for humanity? Or perhaps bewildered about why God would allow this 'major inconvenience' to occur?"

That night I realized that Christ's birth in a stable, inconvenient as it may have seemed at the time, had happened according to God's plan and that God had just as much control over the events happening in my life. This side of heaven I might wonder about my father's acceptance of Christ, but like Mary and Joseph, I was assured that God is in control.

When we left, we stopped at my aide's house so she could follow us to my mother's where I would spend the next few days. Just like Sunday mornings in my growing-up years, we rode in silence until finally, with a heart overflowing with joy, I said, "What did you think of the service?"

"It was very nice, dear," my mother said thoughtfully, "but I'm comfortable with where I am." End of discussion.

The following spring God filled me in on one of the plans He had for me. One Sunday I witnessed my first baptism. While I watched, something inside me stirred and I knew that the time had come.

One month later, Bob Chavez—another "baby Christian"—and I both took the plunge. My decision required the assistance of nearly half the church, plus two home health aides to wrestle my body into dry clothes afterward.

After Sandy drove me to church, we headed backstage. Mae-Lynne, Pastor Keith and a few others hurried over.

"Tim and Bob will carry you up the steps," Pastor Keith said.

"It will be easier for just one person to carry me," I said, envisioning the way Gary used to pick me up with my arm slung around his neck.

Pastor Keith and Sandy, who had already checked out the situation, flashed me knowing looks. "That won't work. The stairs are too narrow."

"Too narrow?"

Sandy nodded her agreement. "One person will need to grab you under your armpits and the other walk in front of you supporting your legs."

I looked up at our assistant pastor. "Bet you never knew this was in your job description, did ya?"

He smiled back. "It goes with the territory."

"We have the church's manual chair waiting for you at the top," Pastor Keith continued. "Bob will help me get it down the steps into the water and back up again. Sandy told me that you catch cold easily, so I turned the temperature of the water up. Did you bring a strap to use as a seat belt?"

"Oh, that won't be necessary," I said. "I can hook my arms behind the push handles to keep from falling forward."

He started to say something, but just then organ music sounded. *Show time!* After a few last minute instructions, the Baker party of many headed toward the steps.

When we got there, I gasped. "Oh, my! I know that Jesus said 'small is the gate and narrow the road that leads to life,' but I never dreamed He was referring to this particular stairway!"

Tim looked over at Pastor Bob. "Ready?"

"Onward and upward."

The two designated carriers picked me up. We made it to the top just fine, where they deposited me in the waiting wheelchair. My fellow "baptizee," Bob Chavez, joined us. He would go first. For some reason, sweat was dripping off his forehead.

While I watched him descend into the water, my mind reeled back to those dark days when I'd wanted to end my life. Since then I'd experienced a complete change of heart—something I could never have pulled off on my own. *Who would have thought that one day I would willingly make a public affirmation of my faith and hand God total control of my life?*

When Bob emerged from the water and climbed the steps, he leaned over and whispered, "All we need are the peas and carrots and we'd have chicken soup!"

I smiled sweetly. "You wouldn't want me to get chilled, now would you?"

Pastor Keith began to speak. "About a month ago Vickie asked me how many people in wheelchairs I'd baptized. I told her she would be my first. Most of you already know about the transformation God has wrought in her life."

At this point he walked toward me and Pastor Bob helped him lower the wheelchair down into the delightfully warm water. Funny, they both had sweat running down their faces too. I hooked my arms around the push handles to keep from toppling forward, but to my amazement, I started floating out of the chair. *No wonder he asked me about a seat belt!*

As my head neared the water, I briefly wondered if I would shortly lose my life, or join the ranks of those blessed few who find it! I could just picture the headlines—"Baptism claims life of drowning victim. . . ." *Get real, Vickie. People don't drown getting baptized.* I smiled, imagining Jesus laughing along with me about this silly notion.

Pastor Keith looked down at me. "Ready?"

I nodded.

"Vickie, do you accept Jesus Christ as your Lord and Savior?"

"I do."

"Do you promise to follow Jesus Christ and to obey His Word to the best of your ability for the rest of your life?"

"I do."

"I now baptize you in the name of the Father, the Son and the Holy Spirit." With that, he placed a handkerchief over my nose.

"Buried with Christ." He tilted the chair back to submerge me. "Risen with Christ, to newness of life."

I did lose my life that day—but I also found it. Coming up out of the water I knew that I no longer ran the show. Somewhere during the last year and a half Jesus had quietly slipped into my heart and become the new Ringmaster. A bold thought entered. *The show must go on, Vickie. If you're willing, now you'll be* My *Little Circus Girl.*

Two weeks later my newfound promise was put to a test. I had wheeled up to my desk to make a phone call, but by the time I hung up, my heart pounded in my ears. Just from hearing the man's name mentioned, five years melted away and I found myself back on the psych ward—helpless, hopeless and in his clutches.

Stop it, Vickie.

Phil, a fellow social work colleague, glanced up. "What's wrong?"

His voice snapped me back to the present. "I—I just called the VA Hospital to check on one of my clients and I found out that's where one of my doctors—I mean, former doctors—is working."

As Phil turned back to his charting, my heart continued to race, my thoughts battling back and forth.

Call him, one side of my brain instructed.

Call him? the other side questioned incredulously.

Look, you've carried these ugly feelings around long enough. It's time to let them go.

Pastor Keith's words during last Sunday's sermon still echoed in my ears. The topic? Forgiveness. Jesus told Peter to forgive not just one or two times, but seventy times seven. To bring closure to that dark era of my life, I knew what I needed to do.

But they were wrong! my mind screamed. *I could have died in that hospital! They never even acknowledged that dysreflexia was a real problem! And they were so patronizing. . . .*

And you weren't? Who is it that lumped them all together under the heading of "god-doc"?

But . . .

And isn't it time you finally admitted to yourself that there was a reason you wound up there? You did *try to kill yourself, remember?*

My thoughts continued to do battle until the realization struck. *Didn't I just promise to follow Jesus Christ and to obey His Word?*

Suddenly, all of those tightly held feelings of resentment seemed childish and petty. Maybe those doctors did lack understanding about my care and maybe their psychiatric treatment did seem less than adequate, but I needed to let it go.

Sitting at my desk I consciously released the anger, resentment and bitterness. No sooner had each doctor's name crossed my lips than the old feelings dissolved like a puff of smoke and the original thought popped back into my mind. *Call him. Tell him how well you're doing. It's time you treated him like you wanted him to treat you—with respect.*

The idea of making this small gesture of goodwill appealed to me. Reaching out, I punched in the number and asked for the doctor by his real name. No more Dr. Gloom—that mythical man belonged to the past.

"Who is this?" said a voice tinged with irritation.

"Um . . . er . . . an acquaintance," I stammered. "Just an old acquaintance."

"He can't talk to you right now. Don't you know he's a very busy man?"

When I hung up, I knew that I would not try to contact him again, but that no longer mattered. In my heart, I had already made my peace. Now it was time to move on.

CHAPTER TWENTY-ONE

The Almighty Cure

◆─◆─◆─◆─◆

Ten, nine, eight . . . Every day at this same time my hearing became highly acute. *Seven, six, five* . . .

Forgetting about the letter I'd spent the last half hour crafting and the phone call I needed to make, I listened for the familiar sounds of a vehicle idling, creeping forward, idling again. *Four, three, two* . . . My hand reached for the power switch on my chair while I peered intently out the window. *Bingo!*

Right on schedule, the white truck turned the corner and slowed to a stop. I backed out of my bedroom, yanked the front door open and cruised down the driveway just as the man with the key opened the locked mailbox. Reaching the sidewalk, I lined up my approach pattern. Don, my mail carrier, looked up and smiled.

"Make it good today, OK?"

"I'll do what I can," he promised as he poked envelopes into the twelve boxes for the complex.

Breathless with anticipation, I leaned forward. When he finished, he reached into my box and placed an impressive stack on my lapboard. "I don't think you'll be too disappointed."

The letter on top made me smile. *Oh good, Willie wrote back. I was getting concerned.* Quickly flipping through the rest, I spotted two more gems with inmate numbers included in the return addresses and a feather-light airmail envelope that hailed all the way from Russia. I seemed to acquire pen pals the way other people collected knicknacks or stamps.

At the bottom of the stack, a fat manilla envelope with the menacing words "Social Services" stamped on it made me cringe. *What do they want now?*

Once I zipped back inside, I decided my phone call could wait. *First things first.* I headed for my latest invention—a new custom-made letter-opener. Hooking a finger through the leather loop, I lifted it to my mouth. Then, clutching the plastic-coated handle between my teeth, I carefully slit each envelope and wrestled the contents out with my teeth.

My writing ministry to inmates had become every bit as exciting as when I reached out to children in our comedy trapeze act. *The pay might not be so hot, but the benefits are out of this world!*

I unfolded Willie's letter. It seemed hard to believe that we had corresponded for over three years now. Willie was doing time behind bars in a harsh Texas prison—his faith never ceased to amaze me.

Hello, my friend. I pray you are up and around and filled with joy. My health is good and my heart and mind are centered on God. . . . I have been trying to come up with the right things to say to a friend who has just observed the tenth year of an accident that altered and changed her life forever. . . . Finally, I prayed and I thanked our Heavenly Father for blessing us with your physical life. . . . [1]

Carefully folding his letter, I popped it in my Important Stuff folder until I could write back. After reading the other personal letters, I took a deep breath and scanned the official Social Services form letter. My heart began to pound as the jarring words leaped off the page.

"We need more information to decide whether your benefits should continue. . . . What is your problem? . . . Contact us immediately to explain your problem!"

I frowned. "You are my problem." The absurdity of it all made me groan. *Lord, please give me patience. Please help me to deal with this senseless bureaucracy yet again. Help me to keep a level head so I can think clearly. I know that murder isn't the best option. . . .*

"Dinner on Wednesday, the 25th?" Virginia repeated over the speakerphone. "I'll have to double-check with Keith, but as far as I know we're free that night."

"Great! May 25th is a very significant date for me."

"Oh? And what's that?" my pastor's wife asked, her voice tinged with excitement.

"It's the tenth anniversary of my accident."

I heard a gasp, followed by dead silence. Finally, a very subdued voice continued. "Will this be a *serious* occasion?"

"No. Not at all. In fact, this year I consider it a celebration."

By the time we hung up, the enormity of what I'd just done shocked me. *Me—inviting people over for dinner? Good luck pulling this one off, Little Circus Girl.*

When my pastor and his wife rang the doorbell on the 25th, they both wore strained expressions, as if they'd just arrived at a wake to pay their final respects.

"Come in!" I said. "Your timing is perfect!"

Pastor Keith's face, bearing an intricate pattern of worry lines, gradually softened. "How so?"

"A friend just finished fixing our dinner and popped it in the oven before she left."

My guests followed me into the kitchen where I put them both to work. Virginia poured dressing on the salad while Pastor Keith pulled out a tray of ice cubes and a pitcher of tea and filled two glasses.

"Aren't you having any?" he asked.

"No," I said, pointing to the cup on my chair. "I've been coughing lately so I have hot tea."

After they carried everything into the dining room, Punkin rubbed up against Virginia's legs. She reached down and scratched his ears.

"Where's Puddin?" she asked looking around for the other cat.

"Probably hiding," I croaked.

"Need a quad cough?" Pastor Keith asked.

"Yes, please." I lowered the back of my chair to a horizontal position. Each time I exhaled, he pushed down on a spot under my diaphragm just below my rib cage. Three or four good strong pushes managed to loosen the secretions.

"That's got it," I said, breathing easier. I pushed the lever to sit back up. "Thank you."

Concern shown in Virginia's eyes. "Isn't it dangerous living here by yourself? What happens if you need help?"

"Oh, that's no problem," I assured her. "I'm actually safer here than I was in the psych ward. I have two great neighbors I can call on in a pinch. Usually one or the other is around. Ever since Gary left, Jeff Miller and Mary Heiderstat have both saved my life on a regular basis."

"Anytime they're not available, will you promise to call me?" Pastor Keith asked.

"Um . . . maybe," I said. "But I still have a problem with that."

"With what?"

"Asking for help. You talked one Sunday about how we need to learn to graciously receive—which is so much harder than giving. At the time, I realized that not only do I have to receive on a regular basis from aides, sometimes I have to ask other people for help—and that's hard. . . ."

Just then the timer buzzed.

Virginia followed me out to the kitchen and carried the bubbling tamale pie back to the table. A savory aroma filled the room. Pastor Keith served each of us. Between bites, conversation continued.

"Did you get your attendant care situation straightened out?" Virginia asked.

"Well, yes and no. I did change agencies. This one doesn't mind if their aides feed my cats, but now I have an afternoon aide who's driving me up the wall! Doing things like changing the sheets isn't on her agenda. She makes me so mad. I realize I'm not supposed to get angry—"

"Who says?" Virginia interrupted.

"Well, it doesn't seem like a very Christian thing—"

Pastor Keith broke in. "Jesus never told us to turn off our emotions. He showed anger."

"He did?"

"Remember when He threw the money changers out of the temple? And when He called the Pharisees a brood of vipers? When your aides aren't doing their job, you need to speak up so you can change the situation."

"Gee, I never looked at it that way before."

Pastor Keith leaned forward in his chair. "Speaking of attendant care, does Gary still do some of your night visits?"

"No. Not since he started school."

"School?" Virginia asked.

"Yeah. He's going for a degree in nursing."

"Do you still keep in touch?"

"Yes. We're still friends. . . ."

When we finished eating, I cleared my throat. "I know that you'd probably agree with my friend Tony that I'm nuts for celebrating this day. As an atheist, Tony is totally baffled by how I can have such an upbeat attitude when viewing life from 'belly button level.' A few years ago he told me that he didn't think he could handle spending his whole life in a chair. I told him that I couldn't either."

Pastor Keith looked puzzled. "Will you explain that?"

"Well, on my own, I can't handle living with a disability. I proved that seven years ago when I tried so hard to kill myself. If life on this planet was all there was, I'd still find it pointless. But God changed that! He's real—and having a personal relationship with Him is out of this world!

"Would you mind if I read you a poem I wrote to commemorate this date?"

"Please do," Pastor Keith said. Virginia flashed me an encouraging smile as I slid the poem out of my folder.

O Little Circus Girl

Back then I idolized
   Flying trapeze,
   Sawdust blazed the trail.
The center ring beckoned,
   Alluring applause,
   So soothing to my soul.

The glitter, the glamour,
   The sparkle, the shine—
   Circus reigned on high!

Sudden the crash,
   The paralyzed limbs,
   Shattered dreams die hard.
Resentment smoldered
   On crumpled wings,
   Splintered my broken heart.
I plummeted down
   My world caved in,
   Secret schemes unfurled.

The anguish, the shock,
   All exit plans blocked,
   My petitions reached Your ears.
Your tender embrace,
   Compassionate love,
   Hope that dried my tears.
Your joy, the flag
   that flies from my heart,
   Glory to the King!

The wonder of dawn,
   Each sunrise a gift
   Reflected in upturned eyes.
Blessings abound,
   My cup runneth o'er,
   Magnificent passion to live!
Thankful my heart—
   A tulip, a rose,
   Blooming in my soul.

O Circus Girl, look—
   the ringmaster changed,
   Now Jesus runs the show.
You celebrate,
   You soar to new heights,
   Abiding in His Word.
Rejoice, O my soul,
   For all to behold,
   Praise to God,
my Redeemer and Lord!

When I finished, I looked up into two smiling faces. "It took me a long time to reach this point," I admitted. "I was so angry at so many people those first years. In the psych ward, I was really mad at God."

Virginia's eyes flashed with questions.

"After the cops hauled me in and I started to believe that God was real, I couldn't imagine why He would allow my brother to die—and me to break my neck. But now it's a little more clear."

"How do you mean?" Pastor Keith asked.

"Well, like Job, I learned that the 'why' is none of my business. God isn't obligated to explain Himself to me. If He was, I guess He wouldn't be God. I might never know the why until I get to heaven, but He has everything under control and that's what counts."

Pausing for a sip of tea, I continued. "Those first years after the accident, I looked to science for the "Almighty Cure." I never thought of turning to God. I thought I couldn't be happy until I was back on my feet, but I've changed my mind. In fact, if doctors came up with a cure tomorrow, I don't know if I'd sign up for it."

"Why's that?"

"Well, in most ways, I've already been cured. Faith might not have changed my circumstances, but it sure has changed me.

"A few years ago in school I made a shocking discovery. I took a test that asked me to write down ten of my favorite activities. To my amazement, seven of them were things I started doing *after* the accident—like my pen pal prison ministry and becoming a professional writer. In fact, there was only one thing on the list that I can't do anymore. Unfortunately, before I got hurt, my whole life revolved around it."

"Trapeze," Pastor Keith said softly.

"Yeah." Keeping a straight face, I added gravely, "I have yet to find a job opening for a quadriplegic trapeze artist."

Catching my humor, he grinned. "That wouldn't surprise me, Vickie. After all, you haven't stopped jumping out of airplanes."

"I still like planting both feet firmly in midair," I admitted, "but nothing compares to the thrill of knowing Jesus Christ.

"Say, are you ready for dessert? I have some delicious peanut brittle in the kitchen."

Pastor Keith smacked his lips. "Need any help?"

"Yes. Would you bring it in? It's on the top shelf of the pantry."

When he left the room, Virginia leaned over and whispered, "That's his favorite. How did you know?"

I shrugged my shoulders. "Just a lucky guess."

Pastor Keith brought the can in, sat down and began to unscrew the lid. Suddenly, he jumped at least a foot in the air, Virginia let out a scream and I casually ducked when the two spring-loaded snakes shot over my shoulder. I couldn't stop laughing.

Pastor Keith smiled sheepishly. "I can't believe I fell for that."

"That makes my whole day. No—that makes my whole week!"

After the delightful evening ended and I lay safely tucked in bed for the night, I marveled to myself. *Quadriplegics aren't supposed to have this much joy, are they?*

In the quiet darkness, a verse I'd read that morning in Psalm 40 sprang to mind. The enormous weight I attributed to these words said it all. "He lifted me out of the slimy pit, out of the mud and mire; he set my feet on a rock and gave me a firm place to stand" (40:2).

Moments later, an enormous weight of a different sort pressed down on me. I gasped. "Punkin—how many times do I have to tell you? You're too heavy to lie on my neck!"

Notes

[1] Letter reproduced with the permission of Willie.

Epilogue

‟This evening I would like to talk to you about peace. The peace that does not depend on circumstances. The peace that is mentioned over 100 times in the Bible. The peace that can only come from having a personal relationship with Jesus Christ.”

When I looked out over the people gathered for the service—patients, their families, hospital staff—I recognized some of the same feelings of despair that I had once felt. Could I help shine a ray of hope into the darkness that clouded those troubled gazes?

Chaplain Rich Stewart, who twelve years earlier had pegged me as the most discouraged, depressed patient he'd ever met, had invited me to speak at Craig Hospital's Christmas Eve service.

"As we prepare to celebrate the birth of Christ," I continued, "I know that many of you may be far from home. Perhaps you're doing time in the hospital. Maybe you're adjusting to the possibility of doing life in a chair. Yet each of you has something very important going for you—something sadly lacking in my life when I did my rehab. You have an interest in God and the faith to be sitting here.

"In 1979 I ran away and joined the circus—literally! I was part of a trapeze act and loved it. Every morning I would mumble to myself, 'People aren't supposed to be this happy when they grow up, are they?'

"Five years later, a split-second mistake in timing dislocated my spinal cord, crumbled my marriage and shattered my career. After my injury, I naively believed all of society's boldface lies about my inferior gimp status. This world, it seemed, did belong to the young, the beautiful and the able-bodied. Crips need not apply.

"For three years, I spent nearly every waking moment reading about cell regeneration and looked to scientists and doctors for the 'Almighty Cure.' Why not? I couldn't perform anymore and I had no desire to do anything else.

"Logically, it made sense to me to end my life. I figured that I'd always need a wheelchair, I'd always be plagued by pneumonia and dizzyingly low blood pressure, I'd always need attendant care—and nothing would ever change.

"Three suicide attempts later, I landed in the psych ward of a local hospital. Late one night in my tiny room, with no place left to run and nothing left to lose, I finally cried out to God.

"The next day, the 'oh my God what am I gonna do' lump in my throat was gone. I've spent the last ten years following my new 'Ringmaster.' Now, I no longer pin my happiness on the hope that I'll rise out of my chair and walk, that I'll regain the use of my hands or that I'll troop with the circus once more.

"I find that the Old Testament prophet, Nehemiah, spoke the truth when he said, 'The joy of the LORD is your strength' (8:10). Joy, to me, is a deep-seated confidence that God is in charge of every area of my life. I don't have to go it alone anymore. . . ."

After the service ended, I met one of the other "Craig survivors" who had spoken during the service about the path that led him to God. Allen, a paraplegic for over ten years, had checked into Craig Hospital five weeks earlier for skin surgery. Since doctors wouldn't allow him up in his chair yet, orderlies had rolled his bed out into the hall—he spoke while lying flat on his back! What a powerful testimony he gave of God's presence—even in the midst of a mandatory two-month stint in the hospital.

When my ride drove me home, a nice surprise awaited me—a Christmas letter from Exodus Prison Ministry confirming that they had reprinted my testimony and sent it out to all 1,500 inmates they work with.

I grabbed a quick bite to eat before my next chauffeur pulled up to take me to the service at my church. That night, Pastor Keith asked some mind-boggling questions.

"What if Jesus hadn't come? What if He hadn't died for our sins? What if there was no eternal hope?"

The thought made me shudder. If that were the case, I would have discovered back in 1987 that there really was no point in sticking around.

When I got home after the service, Gary was waiting for me. He was scheduled to serve as my aide that night. Still an avid trapeze artist, he had arrived early to watch some of the recent practice sessions he'd taped. After he finished with my care, he wanted to watch some of his earlier swings. Over the years, I had saved two video tapes of our trapeze practice. He located them, popped one in and punched "play." Suddenly I found myself jerked back to the very last two-and-a-half I had attempted on the trapeze.

So, at midnight on Christmas Eve, for the first time ever, I watched my head-first plunge into the trapeze net, heard the mournful wail of approaching sirens, saw the big burly paramedics swarming around. This little jaunt down memory lane also slammed home the realization that if not for the accident, I might be merely preparing for the coming of Santa instead of celebrating the birth of our Lord Jesus Christ.

A few moments later, the telephone rang. It was Gary's brother and sister-in-law, Bob and Barb, calling from Virginia to confirm his flight out the next day. Once again I was reminded of God's hand in our lives. If Barb hadn't called the cops on us clear back in Chapter One, we might not even be alive today.

I'm thankful that God does not give up on us even when we give up on ourselves. I know He hasn't given up on Gary either, and I keep praying for the day when we will be brother and sister in the Lord.

Every morning when I awaken, I never know what the day will bring, but I've stopped analyzing God's plan for my life. Receiving a letter from Ringling Bros. & Barnum and Bailey stating that they have an opening for a quadriplegic trapeze artist would not surprise me. I would simply smile, note the opening date and wonder if God's angels were laughing along with Him.

Invitation

❖❖❖❖❖❖

The Joy of the Lord: Unraveling the Mystery

My Personal Journey

Looking for meaning and purpose in your life?

The most exciting thing that I, Vickie Baker, have learned in my journey, is that Jesus welcomes everyone into His kingdom—even you who haven't broken your neck or tried to check out of Life 101. That just happens to be the rocky road that led me to God.

What do I need to do?

Jesus has an entrance exam, but don't worry, you don't need to study for His test. The answer doesn't come from your head—it comes from your heart. In Matthew 11:28 Jesus says, "Come to me, all you who are weary and burdened, and I will give you rest."

Will my problems disappear?

Jesus does not promise that He will take all our problems away. As a matter of fact, I sit at my desk writing these words after having spent six months in bed to heal a pressure sore.

What will happen?

Jesus promises to stay with us when the road gets bumpy, when we get mired in a ditch and are spinning our wheels and even when we lose our way. He specializes in guiding the lost!

Joy

Do you want to be filled with an incredible joy that comes from within? A joy that stays with you— even if your wheelchair and your bottom both break down at the same time? Do you want to have a peace that baffles all human understanding—even in the midst of life's toughest battles? If you answered "yes, yes, yes," you are ready.

COURSE	Eternity 101 with God
RECOMMENDED READING	The Bible—starting with the Gospel of John
AUTHOR AND TEACHER	Jesus
CREDENTIALS	Jesus has taught Eternity 101 since the beginning of time. He wrote the Book! He is the only Instructor who can give you a passing grade.

But I wouldn't qualify . . .

Regardless of your present situation or anything you might have done in the past, Jesus longs for your presence, your companionship and your love. He is waiting for you to ask Him to come into your heart to set up residence. But He will not enter until you ask.

How?

If you have never invited Jesus to be your Savior, you can do so by praying this prayer:

> I, (your name) _____,
> believe that Jesus died on the cross for me and rose from the grave. I believe what the Bible says is true: "For God so loved the world that he gave his one and only Son, that whoever believes in him shall not perish but have eternal life" (John 3:16). Jesus gave His life for me!
>
> I know I've done things that are wrong. *(Be specific and tell God.)* But I want to change. Right now! I want to live a new life. I ask You to forgive me and to be my personal Savior and Lord. Please come and live in my heart. Please change me as Your will unfolds in my life. I can't do it by myself.
>
> Holy Spirit, I invite You to counsel and lead me daily as I call upon You. Be my comforter. Be my companion. Show me Your way.

Thank You, Jesus, for taking the rap for my sins. Thank You for forgiving me and for coming into my life today to run the show.

In Jesus' name I pray, Amen.

Now what?

To find out more about this life-changing decision you have just made, and to answer your "So what in the world do I do now?" questions, you need:

Weekly follow-up

- Sunday worship—find a Bible-believing, Bible-teaching church to join.
- Bible study.
- Friendship with other believers.

Start today!

Someone once said that Bibles should come with a warning label that states, *Caution: Reading this Book can lead to dynamic change. Be prepared for anything!* How true!

In closing, I would like to leave you with this tale:

The Acrobat

One day, a labor strike hit a traveling circus. The owner took seven performers of varying abilities, turned them into acrobats and escorted them up a long ladder to the very top of the tent. Once there, the seven had different reactions.

One spent opening night whimpering that he had never asked to be an acrobat.

Two of them began to argue about the other's qualifications. A fourth angrily told them to be quiet, saying that it hardly mattered since they would all die soon anyway.

The fifth acrobat wasn't so sure. After all, there might be a net down there. Then again, there might not.

The sixth believed that there was a net, but doubted that it was big enough or strong enough to save him. Besides, he wasn't sure that he could actually find the net if he fell.

When the drumroll inevitably came, none of these six left the platform. But the seventh, who knew the Ringmaster personally, had listened carefully to His instructions. On the trapeze and the high-wire he gave such a performance that many children in the crowd decided right then and there to become acrobats.

One day, the drums will roll for each of us. If/when you choose to get better acquainted with the Ringmaster and ask Him to show you how large and strong and secure His net is, you're not a fanatic—just a smart acrobat.

—Author unknown

Annotated Bibliography

◆◆◆◆◆◆

This section contains books that I have found to be helpful in my journey from discouragement, depression and despair to hope, joy and inner peace. While I don't endorse each and every idea presented in these books, it is my hope that you too will find encouragement from them.

Clairmont, Patsy, Barbara Johnson, Marilyn Meberg, Luci Swindoll. *The Joyful Journey*. Grand Rapids: Zondervan Publishing House, 1997.

> *Through the obstacles we sometimes face on life's path, find out how friendships, laughter, love and celebration can bring us closer to God.*

Cousins, Norman. *Head First: The Biology of Hope*. New York: E.P. Dutton, 1989.

> *The author gives scientific proof for something many of us have suspected all along: our moods and attitudes—both positive and negative—biochemically influence our physical health.*

Covey, Stephen. *The 7 Habits of Highly Effective People*. New York: Fireside, 1989.

> *This inspiring step-by-step book contains character-building principles that apply to every area of our lives. Worth putting into practice and periodically reviewing.*

Eareckson, Joni, with Joe Musser. *Joni*. Grand Rapids: Zondervan, 1976.

The remarkable story of Joni's disabling accident at age seventeen and her struggle to adjust, accept and, ultimately, find meaning in life. My role model!

Fulghum, Robert. *All I Really Need to Know I Learned in Kindergarten*. New York: Ballentine Books, 1988.

Prepare to be entertained, uplifted and amused by the profound truth wrapped up in Fulghum's simple statements and witty stories.

Hageseth III, Christian, M.D. *A Laughing Place*. Fort Collins: Berwick Publishing Company, 1988.

One of the worst things that happened to me as a result of my accident was temporarily losing my sense of humor. Learn from an innovative humor theorist the role that humor plays in every aspect of our lives—including illness and wellness.

Hansel, Tim. *Eating Problems for Breakfast: A Creative Guide to Problem Solving*. Dallas: Word Publishing, 1988.

Tim's step-by-step approach to creative problem-solving confirmed my dawning realization that my poor problem-solving skills were not so much due to my disability, as to my attitude. His ideas were a great "Ah, ha!" for me. My other role model!

Kimmel, Tim. *Little House on the Freeway: Help For the Hurried Home*. Portland: Multnomah Press, 1987.

If your life is full to overflowing but you lack inner contentment, this one's for you! Learn the seven marks of a hurried family—and how to change your rushed lifestyle.

Lewis, C.S. *Mere Christianity*. New York: Touchstone, Copyright renewed, 1980.

Do you believe, as C.S. Lewis once did, that there cannot possibly be a good God in light of all the evil in the world? This book is Lewis' forceful and accessible doctrine of Christian belief.

Oech, Roger von. A *Whack on the Side of the Head*. New York: Warner Books, Inc, 1983.

After my accident, I spent four years telling myself, "I can't," and ten minutes figuring out a different way to solve problems. This book helped me to think creatively and learn to do more for myself.

Oliver, Gary, Ph.D. and Norman Wright. *Good Women Get Angry*. Ann Arbor: Servant Publications, 1995.

What? It's OK for women to show anger? This thoroughly biblical and extremely practical book encourages women to own, express and use their anger.

Stanley, Charles. *How to Handle Adversity*. Nashville: Thomas Nelson Publishers, 1989.

Stanley gives practical guidelines to help us respond to adversity, to look at adversity from God's perspective and to discover God's will in each situation. This is one of the most enlightening books I've read on the topic.

Stoop, David. *Self-Talk*. Second edition, Grand Rapids: Fleming H. Revell, 1996.

You will learn the many ways we put ourselves down by our self-talk and how our self-talk can help us gain control of the way we feel and act.

Yancey, Philip. *Where Is God When It Hurts?* Grand Rapids: Zondervan Publishing House, 1990.

What a book! I came away with an understanding of the important role pain plays in our lives and where God really is when we suffer.